Read & Apply to Your life Some

For Luca
May 13, 17

"*I see a young Tony Robbins!*"
- Billionaire Mark Cuban

SELF-MADE SUCCESS

Ivy League Shark Tank Entrepreneur Reveals
48 SECRET STRATEGIES
To Live Happier, Healthier, and Wealthier

SHAAN PATEL
#1 BESTSELLING AUTHOR

Copyright © 2016 by Patel Educational Services, Inc. All rights reserved. Published in the United States of America. Except as permitted under the United States Copyright Act of 1976, no part of this publication may be reproduced or distributed in any form or by any means, or stored in a database or retrieval system, without the prior written permission of the publisher.

Cover Illustrator: Daniel Boom. Cover designer: Sumit Shringi. Editor and interior designer: Danielle Lincoln Hanna.

Enroll in a Self-Made Success Online Course at www.PrepExpert.com

SELF-MADE SUCCESS

SHAAN PATEL

ABOUT THE AUTHOR
SHAAN PATEL

- #1 Bestselling Author
- Winner of *Shark Tank* Deal With Mark Cuban
- Founder of Prep Expert SAT & ACT Preparation
- Perfect-Score SAT Student & Valedictorian
- MD/MBA Student at Yale & USC

Shaan Patel is the founder of Prep Expert SAT & ACT Preparation, a #1 bestselling SAT and ACT book author, and MD/ MBA student at Yale and USC. He raised his own SAT score from average to perfect and teaches students how to prepare for tests using his methods at Prep Expert.

Shaan appeared on ABC's *Shark Tank* to pitch Prep Expert and closed an investment deal with billionaire Mark Cuban. Shaan's newest venture is this book, *Self-Made Success*, and its companion online course that can be found at www.PrepExpert.com.

Dedication

This book is dedicated to all of our students at Prep Expert SAT & ACT Preparation. My favorite part of the business has been hearing from parents and students about how they improved their SAT and ACT scores significantly, got into great universities, and won thousands of dollars in college scholarships. Making a positive difference in students' lives is the best part of my job. I hope *Self-Made Success* will allow me to reach a wider audience to make an even bigger positive impact on more lives.

Contents

INTRODUCTION i
    "I See a Young Tony Robbins." i
    Four Principles of Success iii

CHAPTER 1: UNIVERSAL SUCCESS STRATEGIES 1
    (1) Use the Law of Attraction 3
    (2) Use the Art of Storytelling 11
    (3) Use the Power of Now 20
    (4) Use the Pareto Principle 25
    (5) Use Parkinson's Law 30
    (6) Use the Permission Principle 36

CHAPTER 2: WEALTH SUCCESS STRATEGIES 43
    (1) Realize that Million-Dollar Ideas Are Easy ... 45
    (2) Never Trade Time for Money 53
    (3) Never Expect to Win the Lotto 59
    (4) Be a Big Fish in a Small Pond 61
    (5) Practice Dhandho Philosophy 65
    (6) Capture the Whole Pie 71

Chapter 3: Entrepreneurship Success Strategies — 77
- (1) Do What You Know — 79
- (2) Start a Service-Based Company — 83
- (3) Develop an Unreasonable Obsession — 87
- (4) Just Launch — 91
- (5) Never Go to a Gunfight Without Bullets — 96
- (6) Realize Bureaucracy Is the Root of All Evil — 100

Chapter 4: Social Success Strategies — 109
- (1) It's Better to Be Interested Than Interesting — 111
- (2) Embrace Failure — 115
- (3) Be Fully Transparent — 119
- (4) Play to People's Self-Interests — 122
- (5) Kill with Kindness — 126
- (6) Don't Play the Comparison Game — 133

Chapter 5: Productivity Success Strategies — 137
- (1) Work Smarter and Harder — 139
- (2) Use Internal Motivation — 143
- (3) Start with a Morning Power Hour — 147
- (4) Listen to Audiobooks — 152
- (5) Turn Off the Tech — 158
- (6) Assign Accountability and Deadlines — 163

Chapter 6: Mental Success Strategies — 169
- (1) Practice Self-Control — 171
- (2) Track Progress — 176
- (3) Realize You Are Not This Body … or Mind — 180
- (4) Have Faith — 184
- (5) Treat Entitlement as the Enemy — 188
- (6) Conquer Insomnia and the Fear of Death — 193

Chapter 7: Marketing Success Strategies — 201
    (1) Sell Secrets — 203
    (2) Give Away Free Content — 207
    (3) Be Controversial — 210
    (4) Plant Viral Content — 215
    (5) Be Succinct — 221
    (6) Give People a Bigger Cause — 225

Chapter 8: Academic Success Strategies — 229
    (1) Never Follow Your Passion — 231
    (2) Realize Repetition Is Not the Father of Learning — 234
    (3) Use Tiger Parenting — 238
    (4) Follow the Path of Least Resistance — 242
    (5) Master How to Study — 246
    (6) Go to College … for Cheap — 251

Conclusion — 257
Author's Note — 259

INTRODUCTION

"I SEE A YOUNG TONY ROBBINS."

Billionaire Mark Cuban said the above to me during my pitch on ABC's *Shark Tank*. *Shark Tank* is a television show in which hopeful entrepreneurs pitch their companies to a multibillionaire panel of business magnates for an investment. I went on the show to pitch my test-prep company Prep Expert (formerly 2400 Expert) that offers six-week SAT and ACT prep classes in twenty cities and online. I ended up securing a deal with Mark Cuban for $250,000 in exchange for 20% equity in my company.

But perhaps the ultimate compliment was not Mark Cuban's investment, but what he said about me. He waited until all four of the other Sharks rejected my proposal for an investment to speak about what he envisioned for me. He thought that I was bigger than test-prep and that I would start multiple companies in the future. He said he would like to do an "acqui-hire"—investing in a company to recruit its employees (in this case, me). I said Prep Expert was my "baby." Mark Cuban said he would like to be the "Godfather to my future children."

Mark Cuban gave me the ultimate endorsement. He wanted to invest in me, not just my company. For the record, there's no clause in my contract that states I must give Mark Cuban 20% of all of my future ventures. Instead, it was a handshake deal that I would give Mark Cuban an option to invest in any other company I launch. And why wouldn't I want that option? I believe 80% of any company in partnership with Mark Cuban is more valuable than 100% of a company by myself.

I think Mark saw a little bit of himself in me. Cuban sold his first company, Microsolutions, for $6 million. After taking some time to travel the world, he then started Broadcast.com (formerly Audionet) and sold it for $6 billion to Yahoo! You've got to hit a single before you can hit a home run. Perhaps Cuban thinks that Prep Expert is my single, and he's just waiting to be a part of my home run (*crossing my fingers*).

Mark Cuban also commented that he thought I was a "young Tony Robbins." The comment didn't end up airing on television, but it did serve as the inspiration for this book. If you're not familiar with Tony Robbins, he is the most successful self-help guru in history. His work is inspiring, passionate, and downright life-changing. For Mark Cuban to put me in the same bracket as Tony Robbins is immensely flattering. If *Self-Made Success* can be half as good as any of Tony's books, I'd be elated.

Tony—if you're reading this—I'm a huge fan, and I hope you enjoy *Self-Made Success*!

Some people succeed financially. Others succeed academically. Still others succeed spiritually, mentally, and emotionally. But there are a select few who succeed across all fields—the self-made successes. In this book, I will outline the exact blueprint of how you can achieve success on every level.

By the age of 25, I achieved a perfect SAT score, was valedictorian and homecoming king, received a quarter-million dollars in college scholarships, grew a business from nothing to seven figures from my dorm room, had a multimillionaire Lamborghini-driving business partner, had a multibillionaire NBA-team owning business partner, wrote seven #1 bestselling books, was the youngest recipient of Las Vegas' 40 Under 40 Award, and appeared in over one hundred media and television channels, including *Forbes*, *USA Today*, and *The New York Times*. I did this all while dissecting cadavers at a top-tier medical school in California and attending an Ivy League graduate business school in Connecticut.

So am I just a trust fund baby who was handed a successful business from my parents? No. I have worked for everything I have achieved. Personally, I hate taking handouts. I actually grew up in my parents' urban motel in Las Vegas and attended inner-city public schools in the worst school district in the nation with a 40% dropout rate. The circumstances surrounding your upbringing should not limit you.

So can you really have it all at a young age? Yes. Throw out the conventional wisdom that says you have to pay your dues or climb the corporate ladder. You can have it all and you can have it now. In *Self-Made Success*, I will show you how.

Four Principles of Success

When thinking about how to organize this book, I decided it would be best if I taught the 48 strategies for success the same way that I teach my Prep Expert SAT & ACT Classes. Not only is this teaching method effective, but students also really enjoy it. So I'll follow the same format for this book. Don't worry; you won't get bored.

We use four principles to teach our Prep Expert SAT & ACT Classes: Strategy, Example, Practice, and Review. First, we teach students a particular strategy. Then we show them an example of how to use that strategy on a problem. Next, we have students practice the strategy themselves on questions. Finally, we do lots of review in the course—reviewing previous strategies, problems, and concepts.

Here's how we'll apply this teaching methodology to *Self-Made Success*.

Success Strategy

Success Strategies are the 48 techniques you can use to improve your life.

These are the 48 life lessons that I believe have been most important in helping me achieve success. I developed eight categories with six strategies for a total of 48 strategies:

 (1) Universal Strategies
 (2) Wealth Strategies
 (3) Entrepreneurship Strategies
 (4) Social Strategies
 (5) Productivity Strategies
 (6) Mental Strategies
 (7) Marketing Strategies
 (8) Academic Strategies

The above strategies will teach you how to improve your general, day-to-day life, financial status, entrepreneurial success, social acumen, productive capacity, mental state, marketing prowess, and academic ability. Not every category of strategies may be applicable to you. For example, if you are not in school, then the *Academic Success Strategies* may not be relevant. However, I would still encourage you to read all 48 strategies because there are takeaways from each strategy that can crossover to other parts of your life.

Success Example

Success Examples are illustrative cases of each of the 48 *Success Strategies*.

Lecturing on a particular strategy can get abstract if an example is not given. I use *Success Examples* to show *Success Strategies* in action. I typically will draw examples from my own life, but will occasionally use examples from books, history, or pop culture.

Success Practice

Success Practice includes practical advice on how to apply a particular *Success Strategy* to your own life.

While describing an example from my own life might be interesting to read about, it would be of little value if I didn't teach you how to apply the *Success Strategy* to your own life. *Success Practice* will give you specific tools to implement a particular *Success Strategy* in your own day-to-day life.

Success Review

Success Review goes over previous *Success Strategies* that we have already covered.

This is the fun part—the gamification of *Self-Made Success*. As I write about each technique, I will covertly use a previous *Success Strategy* that we have already covered in the book. It's your job to try to identify which previous *Success Strategy* I am using. Alternatively, I will occasionally ask you to identify where in the book I previously used the current *Success Strategy* that we are discussing. Most people don't remember a concept if they only see it once. I certainly don't. So I will use previous *Success Strategies* as I describe current ones. I hope this will ensure that you don't forget any of the *Success Strategies*. As you read, see if you can identify which previous *Success Strategy* I am using before I reveal it in the *Success Review*.

CHAPTER 1
UNIVERSAL SUCCESS STRATEGIES

(1) Use the Law of Attraction
(2) Use the Art of Storytelling
(3) Use the Power of Now
(4) Use the Pareto Principle
(5) Use Parkinson's Law
(6) Use the Permission Principle

UNIVERSAL SUCCESS STRATEGY #1
USE THE LAW OF ATTRACTION

SUCCESS STRATEGY

The Law of Attraction states that you attract what you think about. You can achieve any goal by visualizing it in your mind, writing the goal down, and positively affirming to yourself that the goal has already been achieved.

I initially came across the Law of Attraction after watching the documentary *The Secret* on Netflix. I then read the book. I read about how different celebrities used the Law of Attraction themselves from Oprah to Richard Gere to Lady Gaga to Jay Z. Perhaps the wildest example that I read about was Jim Carey's use of the Law of Attraction. In 1990 when Jim Carey was still a struggling actor, he wrote himself a $10,000,000 check for "acting services rendered" and post-dated the check for Thanksgiving 1995. Just before Thanksgiving 1995, Jim Carey made $10,000,000 for *Dumb and Dumber*!

Whenever I would read other books, the Law of Attraction kept popping up. I read Jeff Walker's *Launch: An Internet Millionaire's Secret Formula To Sell Almost Anything Online, Build A Business You Love, And Live The Life Of Your Dreams*. Although the book is primarily about Internet marketing, Walker dedicates one chapter to telling readers to write down their goals related to money, relationships, health, and career. I actually followed Walker's advice, and will share with you in the *Success Example* how I already achieved one of the craziest goals I wrote down. Although Walker did not explicitly state that this is the Law of Attraction, concepts such as visualizing goals, writing them down, and believing that they have already been achieved are all attributes of this universal law.

I read Napoleon Hill's classic *Think and Grow Rich*, and once again was amazed that the entire book is about the Law of Attraction—i.e., the thoughts in your mind manifest into reality. Hill describes how famous historical figures such as Thomas Edison, Alexander Graham Bell, Henry Ford, Charles Schwab, Theodore Roosevelt, Woodrow Wilson, William Taft, John D. Rockefeller, and Andrew Carnegie all used the Law of Attraction on the path to success. Hill also does not state that he is talking about the Law of Attraction explicitly, but his principles of desire, faith, autosuggestion, planning, persistence, the subconscious mind, and a definite chief aim are all related to the Law of Attraction.

Here are some great quotes related to the principles of the Law of Attraction.

> *"A man is but the product of his thoughts. What he thinks he becomes."* —Gandhi
>
> *"Whether you think you can or think you can't, either way you are right."* —Henry Ford
>
> *"Nothing is, unless our thinking makes it so."* —Shakespeare
>
> *"If you can dream it, you can do it."* —Walt Disney
>
> *"You become what you think about most of the time."* —Oprah
>
> *"A person is what he or she thinks about all day long."* —Ralph Waldo Emerson
>
> *"Man, alone, has the power to transform his thoughts into*

physical reality; man, alone, can dream and make his dreams come true." —Napoleon Hill

"All that we are is a result of what we have thought. The mind is everything. What we think we become." —Buddha

So how does the Law of Attraction work exactly? First, you need to think of a very specific goal. Then, you need to believe that goal has already been achieved. It's often helpful to do this by visualizing the goal in some way. Finally, you will have to put in effort towards achieving your goal. I don't believe that the universe will just rearrange itself to make your dream a reality. But if you have a concrete goal and you work hard to achieve it, you can expect amazing results.

I won't attempt to claim that I know why the Law of Attraction works. Some experts on the subject claim that our thoughts and feelings have energy and that this energy can be manifested into physical reality. Others believe the Law of Attraction allows us to connect with a higher energy that is within us all—i.e., God. In Hinduism, the word for God is "Krishna," which actually means "all-attractive." To be honest, I have no idea why the Law of Attraction works. But I do know that it works.

You are probably thinking that I am crazy. Most people would dismiss the Law of Attraction as a bunch of garbage. I used to be like you. I didn't think thoughts and feelings have vibrations, that you can achieve anything you believe, or that your mind is the most powerful tool that you have. I've gone to medical school and studied brain physiology deeply, and there's no scientific evidence of the Law of Attraction. But the empiric evidence I have from my own life experiences with the Law of Attraction has convinced me that it is real.

Interestingly, you can use the Law of Attraction without even knowing what it is or realizing that you're using it. Think of a time in your life that you really wanted something badly. Not only did you have a desire for it, but you believed you had already achieved it. You constantly thought about accomplishing this goal and you were obsessed with it. Did it happen? If the answer to this question is yes, you've probably already used the Law of Attraction.

One example from my life is achieving a perfect SAT score. I can distinctly remember in high school thinking about how amazing it would be to get a perfect score on this test. When I started to study for the SAT, I wrote on the front page of my SAT prep notebook that I would get a 2400 on the SAT. I would sometimes daydream about it. I could be walking around my high school, when all of a sudden, I would have an excited feeling come over me and I would exclaim in my mind, "I got a perfect 2400 on the SAT!" This was all before it ever happened.

After I locked myself in the library over a summer and spent hundreds of hours studying for the SAT, I did raise my score from a 1760 to a perfect 2400 on the SAT. Of the 15 million students that took the 2400-version of the SAT, about 3,000 got a perfect score—that's just .02%. Notice that I didn't just think a perfect SAT score would automatically fall into my lap. I certainly worked hard for it. But I had a definite chief aim that I subconsciously believed I had already achieved. Although I didn't know it at the time, I was using the Law of Attraction in high school.

The Law of Attraction does not care how big your goal is. You can have the loftiest ambitions, and the Law of Attraction will help you achieve them. You are really only limited by your thoughts. And most people have many self-limiting beliefs. They think that it would be silly or ridiculous to dream too big. In the *Success Example* that follows, I will share how I achieved one of my biggest goals by specifically using the Law of Attraction.

SUCCESS EXAMPLE

One principle of the Law of Attraction is to write down a goal as if it has already been achieved. So on March 2, 2015, I wrote down the following in a document on my MacBook:

> By the end of 2017, two major accomplishments for me are being selected as *Forbes 30 Under 30* and having Mark Cuban as a business partner.

As I mentioned earlier, I have achieved the latter. I am still working on the former.

I did not go to New York for a *Shark Tank* open call audition until April 9, 2015. So a full month before I even decided to audition for *Shark Tank*, I had written down that I would be business partners with Mark Cuban!

Granted, I was watching *Shark Tank* episodes daily in early 2015. But this further proves my point. You attract what you think about. By visualizing myself on *Shark Tank* every time I watched an episode of *Shark Tank*, I was using the Law of Attraction (without even realizing it).

Skeptics might argue, "Well, you had a definite plan of how you were going to become business partners with Mark Cuban." While this might be true, what are the chances that my plan was going to work? Fifty thousand people audition for *Shark Tank* every year and ten to fifteen will close a deal with Mark Cuban—or .02% (the same chances of getting a perfect score on the SAT).

I had to get through several rounds of auditions including an open call audition, a video audition, and phone audition, just to get a chance to pitch the Sharks. In addition, once I got in the Tank, what were the chances that I was going to land a deal with Mark Cuban rather than one of the other four Sharks? In fact, while I was pitching the Sharks, Mark Cuban was the first one to rip into me saying that, "A new younger guy is eventually going to come in and outwork you." He was clearly disinterested. Then, all of the other Sharks said, "I'm out."

There was a moment in the Shark Tank when I knew that the Law of Attraction is real. With all four of the Sharks out and an unhappy Mark Cuban, my heart was sinking fast because I thought I'd be one of those entrepreneurs who gets quickly booted out of the Tank. But all of a sudden, Mark Cuban looks at all of the other Sharks and asks, "Am I the only one left? Perfect." He then turns to me with a piercing look in his eye. At that moment, I knew the Law of Attraction was real.

What else could explain that the one person in this world that I had written about on March 2nd was now staring me in the face ready to become my business partner on June 24th?

It was the craziest example of the Law of Attraction I had ever encountered.

You might be wondering why all of the other people who think about partnering with Mark Cuban don't have the same success. The Law of Attraction is about more than just thinking about a goal. You have to be obsessed with it, work hard for it, and really feel like you have already achieved it.

SUCCESS PRACTICE

How can you use the Law of Attraction in your own life? There are three key things you need to do in order to use the Law of Attraction:

(1) Write It Down
(2) Add A Deadline

(3) Feel It

First, you need to write your goal down. While thinking about a goal is necessary, writing it down helps with the visualization process. Writing your goal down forces you to be very specific about your goal and helps make it tangible. In 2015, I wrote a "Vision Document" in my MacBook that had goals for each of the following categories:

Happiness
Money
Relationship
Family/Friends
Career
Physical Health
Mental Health
Spirituality
Accomplishments

Create your own Vision Document with goals for each of these categories. Also, be sure to write specific goals as though you have already achieved them. For example, I have a line that says, "I have finally found the love of my life and am engaged to a beautiful, Indian, vegetarian, religious, successful, woman who brings out the best in me." I'm sure my mom is happy about this relationship goal!

Second, you need to set a deadline for your goal. Be reasonable. A goal without a deadline is just a dream. Personally, I would pick a deadline between one and five years. I chose approximately 2.5 years when I created my Vision Document. At the very top of the Vision Document, I wrote "I am 28 years old and by the end of 2017 ... "

Third, you need to feel like your goal has already been achieved. I think Napoleon Hill was incorrect in calling his book *Think And Grow Rich*. A more appropriate name would have been *Feel And Grow*

Rich. A thought without feeling is meaningless. If you don't really believe that your goal is achievable, it won't happen. The most common objection to the Law of Attraction is the following: "So if I just think that I have a million dollars, then I'll have a million dollars—that's garbage!" I agree. Just thinking about a million dollars will not make you a million dollars. Do you currently, at this moment, feel like you already have a million dollars? Or do you currently feel broke? It's the feeling that manifests, not the thought itself.

Success Review

It's a bit hard to review a previous *Success Strategy* here because this is the first strategy in the book. However, I did use the Law of Attraction earlier in the book. Do you remember where? The Introduction.

The very first line of the book is, "I see a young Tony Robbins." This was a vision that Mark Cuban had for me. I could have let his vision vanish by not taking it seriously. Instead, I took it seriously enough that I am now writing this self-help book!

Although I didn't originally have a goal of being a self-help expert like Tony Robbins, Mark Cuban inspired that vision. I then made it a definite chief aim of mine to write this self-help book as the first step on my path to becoming like Tony Robbins. Will the Law of Attraction help manifest my belief that I truly can become similar to Tony Robbins? Only time will tell.

Universal Success Strategy #2
Use the Art of Storytelling

Success Strategy

Storytelling is one of the most powerful ways to connect with your audience. You must learn how to tell stories that are exciting, meaningful, and touching. People love stories.

Storytelling is as old as time itself. Almost every religious text, from the Bible to the Quran to the Bhagavad Gita, is told in the form of stories. Stories can teach us valuable lessons, serve as entertainment, or even offer us an opportunity to transcend our current existence. Two of my favorite Malcolm Gladwell books, *Outliers* and *David and Goliath*, are told through a series of anecdotes. Gladwell is able to connect with millions of readers because he tells interesting stories with powerful takeaways.

But storytelling is not some old pastime that is no longer relevant. Instead, storytelling has become more important than ever today. When you apply to college or grad school, you need to tell a story in the application essay. When you apply for a job, you need to tell stories in your interview. When you pitch an idea or business, you need to tell a story to investors and customers.

In addition, social media has made everyone a content creator. When you post a status update on Facebook, you're telling a story. When you tweet on Twitter, you're telling a short story. When you post a photo on Instagram, you're telling a story. When you create a series of Snapchats, what's that called? Oh that's right—a story.

It's also important how you tell a story. The best storytellers are extremely passionate when they tell an anecdote. When they look you in the eye and use gestures to emphasize points, they are telling the story as much with their body language as they are with their words. Of course, when writing, you don't have the luxury of showing the audience how passionate you are, so you have to tell them.

So what makes a great story? The best stories have three key attributes:

(1) Initial Weakness
(2) Emotional Connection
(3) Powerful Takeaway

A story that has the perfect main character with everything figured out at the beginning would be boring. Instead, people want to see the main character's weaknesses and vulnerabilities initially. Starting a story with an imperfection that your audience can relate to is a good way to bond with your audience. But the story would be no good if it didn't have the main character make progress towards fixing those imperfections. This often gives the audience hope that they too themselves can fix their own imperfections. Beating an initial weakness is a key ingredient in most good stories.

Good stories also create powerful emotional connections with readers. They connect with our universal emotions of love, pain, happiness, hardship, etc. In order to create these connections, the authors of stories need to describe situations and feelings in detail.

Finally, all good stories have a powerful takeaway. This takeaway will often be something that the audience has not thought of before, but finds to be true. Typically, the audience is convinced that the universal takeaway is true because they have an example in front of them as evidence—the story itself. Note that the takeaway does not necessarily need to be explicitly stated; it can be implicitly embedded in the story itself.

Success Example

Here are just a few examples of how I have practically used the Art of Storytelling in my own life:

> **(1) College and Scholarship Essays** — When applying to colleges and scholarships, I wrote a story about how my upbringing in a motel helped me appreciate diversity.
> **(2) Med School Interviews** — When interviewing for med school, I told a story about how my experience volunteering in an emergency department sparked my interest in the field of medicine.
> **(3) Literary Agents** — When I wanted to publish my first SAT prep book, I e-mailed a story to literary agents about why I was the perfect person to write the book.
> **(4) Media** — When I wanted to get media coverage, I e-mailed reporters the story they should consider writing.
> **(5) Med School Notes** — When I needed to write notes for patient medical records as a med student, I had to tell a story about the patient's medical history.
> **(6) Business School Cases** — When I needed to write case analyses as a business school student, I had to tell a story about the company's problem and how they could solve it.
> **(7) *Shark Tank*** — When I wanted to get on *Shark Tank*, I pitched a one-minute short story at the audition to casting call producers about why my company was perfect for the show.

Perhaps the most important storytelling I have ever done though has been related to my business. I integrated my personal story of struggling with the SAT directly into my business Prep Expert. I used to dislike the fact that Prep Expert is so attached to me as the founder. Not only does it make the company virtually impossible to sell (not that I want to), but I also thought it makes the company less professional since Princeton Review and Kaplan are faceless. However, we've found that students love having a tangible story they can relate to. Using a powerful, personal story is actually a great way to start a business!

I personally struggled with the SAT, but through focused preparation was able to raise my own score from average to perfect, which resulted in acceptances to prestigious universities such as Brown, Northwestern, and UC Berkeley; a quarter-million dollars in college scholarships from companies such as Coca-Cola, Toyota, and McDonald's; and even the opportunity to meet the President of the United States. My personal story helps inspire students to work hard in our courses and achieve their own college and scholarship goals.

Here is my personal story:

> I grew up in a cramped two-bed, one-bath living space in my parents' rundown Las Vegas motel frequented by drug addicts, prostitutes, and police. I remember walking as a six-year old in flip-flops along my cracked "neighborhood" sidewalk trying to avoid shattered glass from broken beer bottles. Although too embarrassed to invite friends over, I was lucky enough to have loving parents who adhered to Indian cultural values of tolerance, hard work, and most importantly education. My mom would say "two things—school and food—we'll spend money."

> After volunteering at a local emergency department, I was inspired to become a physician. I became intrigued with combined baccalaureate/MD programs that offered high school students a guaranteed spot in medical school. However, these programs had an average acceptance rate of 5% and SAT score of 2250. After receiving a 1760 on my first practice SAT, I spent countless hours studying at the library to raise my score to a perfect 2400. But my reluctance to share the upbringing I had been ashamed of as a

child led to sub-par applications that didn't truly convey my personal story. Despite multiple rejections, my acceptance into the USC Bacc/MD program on a full scholarship made the other disheartening envelopes disappear.

Because students in Bacc/MD were encouraged to explore interests outside of medicine, I pursued writing an SAT prep book to help other students prepare for the SAT the way that I did in high school. Unfortunately, most literary agents and publishers dismissed my book proposal, with one stating, "I didn't find Shaan's writing or persona particularly engaging—he's not a great writer, no matter what his score is." After writing hundreds of pages, I had two options: continue to hope for a book deal or give up. But when life gives you Plan A or Plan B … make Plan C. I used extra scholarship money I had saved as initial capital to launch Prep Expert SAT Prep. The 376-point average score improvement in the pilot class confirmed that my "easy-to-read" text which publishers had criticized actually resonated quite well with high school students.

When McGraw-Hill saw what I was building, the acquisitions editor offered me a book deal. What I had originally wanted didn't become a reality until I proved my expertise elsewhere. Ironically, I spent just as many hours in the same library during the summer of 2011 writing an SAT prep book as I did during the summer of 2006 studying for the SAT. The only difference was that in 2006 I was solely concerned about my own future, whereas in 2011 I was concerned about the future of thousands of students.

During medical school at USC, I wanted to develop an online SAT course. But there was one central challenge: McGraw-Hill now owned the copyright to my material. When I began contacting online test prep providers, one potential partner said, "It won't be possible to use that material in online SAT prep … you've backed yourself into a corner." But I didn't let this defeatist attitude stop me from finding a trapdoor escape out of that corner. After *meeting the founders of Veritas Prep, we pursued literary licensing until negotiations became stagnant. I then reached out to McGraw-Hill's VP of Global Sales directly and outlined how packaging every online course with a copy of my book SAT 2400 in Just 7 Steps would help sell thousands of more books than projected—and he approved the deal!*

I continued to challenge defined limits by taking a leave of absence from med school at USC to attend business school at Yale for a dual purpose: to learn more about healthcare management and to scale my company from a small business in Las Vegas to a national test-prep brand. Not only have I achieved both goals, but I also appeared on ABC's Shark Tank in January of 2016. The publicity from Shark Tank as well as strategic partnership with Mark Cuban has transformed my business. We truly are on our way to becoming one of the nation's largest test-prep companies.

I certainly could've taken the road well-travelled and sat on my perfect SAT score. But I found an empty market niche and leveraged my assets to develop an effective curriculum that helped students improve their academic futures.

Never let someone tell you that you can't do something. The negativity someone projects on you is just a reflection of the fears that they latently harbor themselves.

Let's do a quick check. Does my story have all three key attributes of a compelling story?

(1) Initial Weakness — Yes. I share how I initially faced many rejections on my path to SAT, scholarship, business, and book success.
(2) Emotional Connection — Yes. I make emotional connections when I share my experience growing up in my parents' motel.
(3) Powerful Takeaway — Yes. I teach my audience how success

is possible no matter how many times you are rejected.

SUCCESS PRACTICE

Now let's talk about how you can master the Art of Storytelling.

Use the Situation-Task-Action-Result (**STAR**) model when sharing stories.

Situation — the background context
Task — the primary issue
Action — the action taken
Result — the ultimate outcome

Following the STAR model is a surefire way to craft a powerful story. In the *Success Example*, notice how I used this model:

Situation — I wanted to write an SAT prep book
Task — I needed to get a literary agent and publisher
Action — I started my own test-prep company
Result — I was able to generate great results for students despite initial rejections

Mastering the Art of Storytelling also requires that you write well. You don't have to be a superb writer in order to tell great stories. In fact, I'm sure you've noticed that I am not the best writer. Instead, I write how I speak—using simple, colloquial language.

But learning how to write decently well was certainly the most important skill I learned in high school. Although my education has always focused on science and business, writing has been the central thread that has been essential to all aspects of my career.

If you don't think you are a good writer, one thing you can do is tape yourself talking. Then simply write down what you said and clean it up a bit. This is actually how I wrote my New SAT books. Instead of writing the books, I taught the strategies in a video course first. I then just watched the video course and wrote down what I said to put together my New SAT books. I found this to be a very good way to bypass the arduous task of writing.

But there really is no replacement to taking a writing course with a good English instructor. I am so thankful to my AP English teachers from high school (Mr. Blank and Mrs. McCoy) for building my writing foundation. Although I remember being near tears when Mr. Blank once crossed out half of one of my essays after I had spent eight hours working on the composition, I now appreciate all of the writing iterations he forced me to make. To become better at writing, you must practice, practice, practice. I used to think that most of the essays we wrote in high school and college were a waste of time. Little did I know that all of that practice would serve me very well in my career. I now use the writing skills that I learned in high school and college to write blog posts, business proposals, media pitches, patient medical notes, case write-ups, and even this book!

SUCCESS REVIEW

Which previous *Success Strategy* did you notice while I was discussing this one?

Use the Law of Attraction

I used the Law of Attraction to get into the baccalaureate/MD program at USC that I mentioned in the *Success Example*. In high school, I was obsessed with getting into one of these programs. I knew that I wanted to go to med school but I didn't want to play the premed rat race. Guaranteed admission into medical school meant that I wouldn't have to worry about keeping a super high GPA in college, getting a high MCAT score, doing research, volunteering at hospitals/overseas, going through the med school application and interview process, etc.

I envisioned myself having a very relaxing and fun undergrad experience since I knew that I would have to buckle down again in med school—and that's exactly what happened. Despite the low acceptance rates to baccalaureate/MD programs (less than 5% at most universities), I got into four programs—USC, Northwestern, Boston University, and Villanova. I chose USC because they also gave me a full-tuition scholarship.

I did not envision myself at Harvard, Princeton, or Stanford. If I went to any of these schools, I would have had to battle it out as a premed. If I had been obsessed with going to an Ivy League university (or Stanford), I'm sure the Law of Attraction would have made it possible. But I simply wasn't interested in that.

UNIVERSAL SUCCESS STRATEGY #3
USE THE POWER OF NOW

SUCCESS STRATEGY

The secret to happiness is to focus on the present moment. Most stress is caused by anxiety about the future or regret about the past. By living in the present, rather than the past or the future, you can eliminate worry from your life.

Eckhart Tolle's *The Power of Now* changed my life. Tolle is one of the most celebrated spiritual leaders in the western world, but many of his teachings derive from eastern philosophy. In his book *The Power of Now*, Tolle asserts, "Nothing has happened in the past; it happened in the Now. Nothing will ever happen in the future; it will happen in the Now." If you focus on the present moment, you should not worry about what happened yesterday nor should you be anxious about what will happen tomorrow.

The concept of focusing on the present moment is not limited to Eckhart Tolle's teachings. In fact, one of the greatest self-help experts of all time, Dale Carnegie, also knew this secret. Most people know Dale Carnegie as the author of *How To Win Friends And Influence People*. However, Carnegie also wrote an equally good book called *How To Stop Worrying And Start Living*. In the book, Carnegie asserts that, "The load of tomorrow, added to that of yesterday, carried today, makes the strongest falter. Shut off the future as tightly as the past. The future is today. There is no tomorrow. The day of man's salvation is now." Notice any similarities between this quote from Carnegie and the previous quote from Tolle? Carnegie also encourages his readers to live in "day-tight compartments"—to not worry about yesterday or tomorrow, but to focus on the present-day only.

To focus on the now is not easy. Our minds are constantly running between the past and the future, but hardly ever enjoying the present. You must train your mind to focus on the present moment in order to be truly happy.

Social media has made focusing on the present an especially difficult task. It's so easy to open Facebook, Twitter, Instagram, or Snapchat and observe happy moments that others are having. This can decrease your own happiness because you regret that you didn't take part in those past moments or worry that you won't have similar moments in the future. Do not worry—social media posts are unrealistic snapshots of an always-exciting life that no one possesses. You can immediately supersede the happiness of all social media posts by enjoying the current moment, whether it is exciting or not.

If you are a "what-if" person, then focusing on the now can be particularly difficult. My mom is a "what-if" person. She worries about all kinds of future scenarios: What if my dad never retires? What if Shaan doesn't find a good wife to marry? What if she has a major health problem? All of these "what-ifs" are pointless to think about because they all occur in imaginary scenarios within my mom's mind's future. To stop worrying, enjoy the present moment. The future will work itself out—no "what-ifs" necessary.

There are two groups of people who are really good at using the Power of Now: children and drug addicts. Adults often wish they could be as carefree as children. I have good news for you—you can! All you have to do is focus your mind on the current moment. That's it. Children are good at not caring about what happened yesterday or worrying about what's going to happen tomorrow. You should too.

Drug addicts are also good at focusing on the present moment ... when they're on drugs. One of the biggest appeals of drugs is that they can help us experience moments more fully. But what if you could do so without the drug? I have more good news for you—you can! I will outline some techniques you can use to enjoy a drug-free present moment in the *Success Practice* section.

Success Example

As a medical student, I was often unhappy. I would be stressed about the next exam, downtrodden after a surgeon just yelled at me in the OR, or worried that I may not match into the residency of my choice. These are just some of the feelings that doctors-in-training experience every day.

Becoming a physician is no easy task. In the United States, it often takes 11 to 15 years of education after high school: four years of college, four years of medical school, and three to seven years of residency. Along the way, you are faced with competitive admission committees, difficult exams, and uncertainty of whether you will make it all the way through.

Why put up with all of this stress and anxiety? Because young doctors are often looking forward to a "good life" later on. Not only are doctors viewed as financially well-off, but they are also among the highest respected professionals in society. Therefore, we deal with what we have to in order to become physicians.

The promise of future salvation is what keeps us going. However, now that I've had a chance to take a leave of absence from medical school for two years to pursue an MBA, I got the opportunity to reflect on the past three years of my medical school career. Here is the secret to why so many future—and present—doctors are unhappy:

There is no such thing as future salvation.

Eckhart Tolle's *The Power of Now* stresses that if you are always looking forward to happiness in the future, then you will never be happy at all. You can only be happy in the now. If you are not happy now, then don't expect to be happy later. Be happy now or be miserable forever.

But searching for future salvation is exactly what medical students, residents, and even physicians do. We are willing to put in the time and energy to become physicians because of the idea of delayed gratification. We'll work our tails off now so that later we can live a life in which we can provide great care to our patients, get paid well for doing it, and live a more balanced life.

But that is a flawed mentality. I realize now that I was always looking forward to getting something over with in medical school: the next block of curriculum, the next United States Medical Licensing Exam, the next clinical rotation, etc. Once I got done with that one thing, I would hope that my life would be a little better. But it wasn't.

And that is what we, as future physicians, do. We expect that life will be better once we are done with premed, medical school, and residency. But it doesn't get better. It will stay the same … unless you change your mentality.

Enjoy the now. Enjoy studying for the organic chemistry test if you are a premedical student. Enjoy rotating through general surgery as a medical student. Enjoy working 80-hour weeks as a resident. If you do not enjoy your current situation, you will not enjoy your future one.

Be happy now. It is the only way to be happy ever.

SUCCESS PRACTICE

Okay, while it's great to have an academic understanding of the Power of Now, how can you practically apply it? The problem with focusing on the present moment is that it's easy to say, but hard to do.

Here's one practical technique that I use to apply the Power of Now. Stop and observe the thoughts in your mind! Examine what you are thinking about. Are you thinking about something that occurred in the past or something that might happen in the future? If the answer is yes, then you need to refocus on the present moment. To do this, use your five senses:

> **(1) Sight** — What are you looking at right now? Don't just name what you're looking at. But really observe and appreciate it.
> **(2) Touch** — What are you touching right now? Focus on different body parts. Observe what your hands are feeling, what your feet are feeling, how the air you are breathing feels inside your lungs as you inhale and exhale.
> **(3) Smell** — What are you smelling right now? If there isn't in a specific smell, appreciate the clean air that you are taking in through your nose.
> **(4) Taste** — What are you tasting right now? If you aren't eating or drinking anything right now, take a sip of water and observe how it tastes.
> **(5) Hear** — What are you hearing right now? If it's your favorite song, turn it up and really enjoy it. If it's completely silent, enjoy the silence.

Now, return to your mind. More often than not, the worry that plagued your mind previously has vanished. It feels like a weight has been lifted off of the shoulders of your mind. Try this mind hack out and see if using the Power of Now works for you.

Success Review

Which previous *Success Strategy* did you notice while I was discussing in this one?

Use the Art of Storytelling

In the *Success Example*, I shared a story about my medical school experience. Let's see how well the story fulfills the three key attributes of a compelling story:

(1) Initial Weakness — Yes. I share that I was often unhappy in medical school.
(2) Emotional Connection — Yes. I make an emotional connection around fear.
(3) Powerful Takeaway — Yes. I teach my audience how they don't need to change anything they're doing in order to be happy, but just change how they think about what they're doing.

Let's also determine whether I used the STAR Model:

Situation — I want to become a physician.
Task — I need to go through an enormous amount of training to become a physician.
Action — I begin to appreciate the journey more than the outcome.
Results — I am now happy as a med student without changing anything other than my mindset.

Master the Art of Storytelling—it will serve you well in every endeavor you ever pursue.

Universal Success Strategy #4
Use the Pareto Principle

Success Strategy

The Pareto Principle states that 80% of all results are due to 20% of all causes. It is also known as the 80/20 Principle. Take advantage of the Pareto Principle to succeed in all aspects of life.

In 1896, Italian economist Vilfredo Pareto found that 80% of the land in Italy was owned by 20% of the population. He also found that 80% of the peas in his garden came from 20% of the peapods. From these observations, he developed a mathematical Pareto distribution that shows the 80/20 Principle to hold true across many disciplines—business, economics, science, software, healthcare, etc.

In business, 80% of revenue comes from 20% of a company's products. For example, at Prep Expert, we have five major service offerings: SAT Prep Courses, ACT Prep Courses, Private Tutoring, Weekend Camps, and College Admissions Consulting. However, sales are not split evenly among the five product categories above. Due to the Pareto Principle, 80% of our revenue comes from SAT Prep Courses, which makes up 20% of our service offerings.

The most important takeaway from the Pareto Principle is to realize that all effort is not rewarded equally. Once you realize this misdistribution of effort and reward, you need to figure out how to best allocate the limited resources you have (primarily time and effort) to yield maximum results.

SUCCESS EXAMPLE

The Pareto Principle actually manifested itself on national TV for me. On ABC's *Shark Tank*, I initially asked for $250,000 in exchange for 10% equity of Prep Expert. Mark Cuban gave me a counter-offer of $250,000 in exchange for 20% equity of my company. After some weak negotiating on my part, Mark Cuban would not budge from the 80/20 split. He also suggested an 80/20 split for all of my future companies.

Given that I knew before stepping into the Tank that the maximum equity I would be willing to give up was 20%, I had no problem accepting his offer. I look at it in terms of total value. Is a company more valuable if I own 100% of it on my own or is it more valuable if I own 80% of a company with Mark Cuban? I think it's the latter.

I believe that the 20% Mark Cuban and *Shark Tank* bring to my company will generate 80% of all future revenue. Mark Cuban's brand, network, experience, and team bring a tremendous amount of value to Prep Expert. In addition, the publicity from yearly *Shark Tank* updates because we are a Mark Cuban Company is an added bonus. There is no doubt in my mind that 80% of my company's revenue is due to Mark Cuban and *Shark Tank*—the Pareto Principle is in full effect.

SUCCESS PRACTICE

For business owners, let's examine your revenue and products. Analyze your accounting books to determine which 20% of your offerings are generating 80% of your revenue. Now, maximize those products. Determine if there are opportunities to sell more of the thing you sell best. If you don't already, can you offer your product online? Can you make it easier to purchase for customers? Can you lower the price to sell a greater volume? Can you bundle other products with your main product as an add-on? Figuring out how to sell more of your bestseller can dramatically increase your business.

For non-business owners, let's examine your paycheck and workload. List the five tasks that you do most at your job. Determine which one of these five tasks generates 80% of your value to the company and 80% of your recognition by superiors. Now, optimize this task. Can you do this task better? Can you do this task faster? Are there web tools available to help you automate this task? Can you dedicate less effort to tasks that don't matter as much? Increasing your efficiency in the workplace using the Pareto Principle can significantly benefit your career.

For students, let's examine your grade and effort. List the five tasks that you do most in a particular class. Determine which one of these five tasks generates 80% of your grade. Even if your class syllabus says that the grade will be based 25% on participation, 25% on homework, 25% on tests, and 25% on a final presentation, you should not spread your effort evenly across these four categories. Instead, you should figure out which categories will require the most and least effort to score well in and spread your effort out accordingly. The trouble so many students have with academics is not knowing how to allocate their effort. If you work hard on everything, especially on assignments that don't mean much to your grade, you can quickly burn out. Use the Pareto Principle to become an efficient student.

SUCCESS REVIEW

Which *Success Strategy* did you notice while I was discussing this one? Actually, it would be impossible for you to notice. But this book itself is actually a manifestation of the Pareto Principle.

Self-Made Success took me approximately ten weeks total to write. However, I wrote the bulk of it in two weeks. Essentially, 20% of the time that I allotted to writing *Self-Made Success* produced 80% of the content in the book.

I had to write most of this book in two weeks not by choice, but out of necessity. I originally thought that I could write chapters of *Self-Made Success* regularly over ten weeks while I was completing my last semester of business school at Yale. But it turns out that it's rather difficult to write a book while being in graduate school and running a growing company.

So I dedicated my entire two-week Spring Break to writing *Self-Made Success*. Writing for eight hours a day for fourteen days straight is probably not what most people think of when they think of Spring Break. But I'm willing to bet that 20% of *Self-Made Success* readers would be willing to sacrifice their Spring Break to work on a project they're passionate about!

Universal Success Strategy #5
Use Parkinson's Law

Success Strategy

Parkinson's Law states that "work expands to fill the time available for its completion," or that "work contracts to fit in the time we give it." If you have a month to complete a task, the task will take a month to complete. If you have a day to complete the same task, the task will take a day to complete. Use Parkinson's Law to get more done by allotting less time to tasks.

I bet you have unknowingly used Parkinson's Law before. Have you ever been given a few months to write a paper for a class in school, only to spend the night before it is due completing the entire paper? This is Parkinson's Law at its finest. The work of the paper contracted to fit within the one day of time you gave it. If your teacher had given you one week, instead of a few months, to complete the paper, much of the class would have complained. But the paper would have gotten done regardless due to Parkinson's Law.

Parkinson's Law most often manifests when you think you have too much to do in too little time. More often than not, no matter how much work you have to do or how little time you have, you accomplish what you need to. For example, in the summer of 2011, I had two months to write my book *SAT 2400 In Just 7 Steps* for McGraw-Hill before I started medical school in August. I felt completely overwhelmed. Not only was this the first time that I was writing a book, but it just seemed like there was too much to write in too little time. But every day for 80 days, I chipped away. I spent twelve-hour days in the library writing. I finished the book the day before I started medical school.

One potential danger of pushing Parkinson's Law to the extreme is diminishing quality. You might think that the quality of work suffers if it is given too little time to be completed. I don't believe this to be true. As long as you are reasonable about the time you allot a certain task, the quality hardly diminishes at all. This is the beauty of Parkinson's Law. For example, *SAT 2400 In Just 7 Steps* sold over 30,000 copies, received great reviews, and was even a #1 bestseller on Amazon for SAT prep.

Parkinson's Law teaches us one key lesson: don't give yourself too much time for any amount of work. If you allot yourself too much time for a task, you are wasting time. If you allot yourself too little time for a task ... well, there is actually no such thing. Parkinson's Law will assure that you get any amount of work done in the allotted time, no matter how much work you have or how little time you have.

SUCCESS EXAMPLE

I used Parkinson's Law to study for two graduate school admissions exams: the MCAT and the GMAT. The MCAT is the five-hour Medical College Admissions Test required for admission into medical school in the United States. It tests general chemistry, organic chemistry, physics, biology, and verbal reasoning. The GMAT is the Graduate Management Admission Test required for admission into business school in the United States. It tests quantitative skills, verbal reasoning, integrated reasoning, and writing ability.

Self-Made Success

Most students spend 200 to 300 hours studying for the MCAT over three to six months. I used Parkinson's Law to study for the MCAT in six days.

During the summer after my sophomore year of college, I wanted to take the MCAT so that I wouldn't have to worry about it junior year. Therefore, I scheduled to take it at the end of summer just a few days before school would resume.

However, I simply could not get myself to study at all during the summer. This was primarily due to the cushy requirements of the Baccalaureate/MD program I was enrolled in at USC. The program only required that I score a 27 on the MCAT (out of 45) in order to be guaranteed acceptance into medical school. This was especially nice because a 27 on the MCAT was around the national average, but the average MCAT score of students who were accepted to medical school at USC through the traditional application route was 34.

So all I had to do was score a 27. But I spent the summer in LA taking a physics class at USC, and could not bring myself to study for the MCAT for the life of me. I flew back home to Las Vegas (where I had registered to take the MCAT) near the end of summer and that was it: I now had six days before the MCAT and I hadn't studied at all.

I took a practice MCAT to get a baseline score—I got a 21. I had six days to raise my MCAT score 6 points. I buckled down and got to work. After spending six twelve-hour days in the library studying for the MCAT, I then took the MCAT officially. My score came back a few weeks later and I got a 30. This was comfortably a few points higher than the minimum 27 score I needed for my medical program.

This was one of the craziest examples of Parkinson's Law I had ever seen. I had planned to study for the MCAT all summer. Instead, I studied for just one week. And I did just fine. The studying of the MCAT reduced to fit within the time that I gave it.

I went through a very similar situation when applying for my MBA. Because I was in medical school, I didn't have much time to study for the GMAT. Most students spend 100 to 200 hours studying for the GMAT over three to six months.

But given my past experience with the MCAT, I decided to study for another graduate admissions exam in one week again. So I spent the spring break of my second year of medical school studying twelve hours a day for the GMAT. I was able to raise my score from a 680 to a 750 (out of 800) and was admitted to the Yale School of Management. Once again, Parkinson's Law reduced the work down to the time I allotted it.

Success Practice

Is Parkinson's Law just a universal force that you can't practically apply to your own life? No. You can consciously practice using Parkinson's Law. When you begin to use Parkinson's Law, you will accomplish twice as much in half the time.

To use Parkinson's Law, you need to create self-imposed deadlines. Think of a particular task you need to complete. Estimate how long you think it would take to complete this task. Now, I want you to cut that time in half. Make this your own self-imposed deadline to complete the task. While you might think that it's impossible to complete the task within this short of a timeframe, do not worry. When you give yourself so little time, some anxiousness is expected. But really stick to the self-imposed deadline. You will amaze yourself with how much work you can get done when you just give yourself less time.

It's almost impossible to allot yourself too little time for a task. Challenge yourself by giving yourself what seem like impossible deadlines to meet, and you will be surprised at the magic Parkinson's Law produces.

For example, let's say you have a goal of losing ten pounds. A typical person might think that this would take three months. Now, I want you to give yourself six weeks. Essentially, you'll need to lose a pound every four days. Do everything you need to hit that goal (barring unhealthy behaviors such as starvation or purging). Exercise more, eat fewer calories, weigh yourself daily, etc. You will surprise yourself! Not only will you likely lose ten pounds in six weeks, but you will also pick up lots of healthy diet and exercise habits along the way.

Once you begin to use Parkinson's Law, you will eventually be able to push it to extremes you never thought possible.

Success Review

Where in this book did I implicitly mention that I was using Parkinson's Law? In the last *Success Review,* I mentioned that I am writing 80% of *Self-Made Success* in two weeks. So this book is not only a manifestation of the Pareto Principle, but also of Parkinson's Law.

My first book took me about ten months to write (with about 80% of it being written in two months). My next few books took me about one to two months to write. For *Self-Made Success*, I thought, why not push Parkinson's Law to its extreme? I'll write *Self-Made Success* in just two weeks.

You be the judge. Do you think the quality of *Self-Made Success* suffered because I decided to write 80% of it in two weeks? Or is this book an example of practicing what I preach? Use Parkinson's

Law to accomplish more than you could have ever imagined in less time than you ever thought possible.

Universal Success Strategy #6
Use the Permission Principle

Success Strategy

The Permission Principle is just a term that I made up. It derives from the age-old adage, "It's better to ask for forgiveness than permission." If you are constantly asking for permission, you will drown in a sea of "No's." To practice the Permission Principle, don't ask for permission.

Almost every time I have asked for permission from people in positions of power, I am met with a resounding "No." Authority causes people to have inflated egos. Policies stifle creativity. Combine the two and you have a dangerously inhibitive mixture.

By asking for permission to carry out an objective, you give authorities the opportunity to exercise their power. And when people have a chance at power, they seize it. More than likely, the authority will prevent your action from getting done at all, or best-case scenario, delay it tremendously.

Instead, try carrying out an action without telling the authority. I have noticed one of two things typically happens. Either the authority doesn't notice that you even took the action or the authority may slap your wrist. But if you played within the rules, the authority can't do much about it. You can then ask for forgiveness. By asking for forgiveness, you are usually in a much better position than you would have been if you had asked for permission.

Of course, you need to be careful when using this strategy. You don't want to move forward with an action that would cause you to break the law or do something wholly unethical. But you should consider bending the rules. Even if you are reprimanded afterwards, if the benefits outweigh the costs—go for it.

SUCCESS EXAMPLE

School is the perfect example of a bureaucratic organization that is good at denying permission. Here's one example of how I used the Permission Principle to bypass the authority and policies of school administration.

After I completed my first year of business school at the Yale School of Management (SOM), I knew I had my work cut out for me over the summer. No, I was not going to do a finance or consulting internship like most of my classmates. Instead, I was headed back to Las Vegas to work on my business, Prep Expert.

I had five main objectives during the summer of 2015:

(1) Write five New SAT books (1,000 pages of content)
(2) Develop a new curriculum for our SAT prep courses for the New SAT coming out in 2016
(3) Open twenty New SAT test center locations across the country
(4) Hire and train over twenty instructors and test proctors in each new city
(5) Prepare our company for the *Shark Tank* Effect (i.e., optimize sales, operations, marketing, business development, website, etc.)

This was an overwhelming amount of work I was trying to complete in a short, three-month summer. I knew I needed more time. So I came up with a plan. I simply wouldn't register for any classes in the first quarter of the fall at Yale. This would allow me to extend my summer from three months to five months. And I would still have enough credits to graduate because I had taken extra classes during my first year of business school. It was the perfect way to extend my summer in order to work on my company and still get my MBA degree.

But I made the mistake of asking for permission. I met with the Dean of Academic Affairs at Yale, and she told me there was a "policy" that would prevent me from carrying out my plan. She said that all Yale MBA students have to be enrolled in four classes every quarter and take 16 credits worth of classes every semester, regardless of whether they have enough credits to graduate. Well, that certainly ruined my day.

So I did what any person who follows the Permission Principle would do, and stopped asking for permission. I looked up all of the online classes I could take at Yale. I found a few and enrolled in all of them so that I could take Yale classes remotely from Las Vegas. But I still faced a couple of challenges.

Although the second year of business school at Yale SOM is almost entirely elective, there was one required leadership class that met five times in New Haven and students were required to attend. If I didn't pass this class, I wouldn't graduate. Once again, I made the mistake of asking for permission with the following e-mail to the professor who taught the leadership class:

> *Hi Professor XXXXX,*
>
> *I am currently registered for MGT-432 Leadership Practicum in Section 05. However, my summer internship has required me to stay through Fall 1 on the west coast. Therefore, I am doing a remote Fall 1 semester through Yale online classes and independent studies.*

I was wondering if I could fly in for a couple of the in-person classes for the Leadership Practicum, and do makeup assignments for the ones I miss? Flying in for every in-person meeting would be very costly for me. For example, could I fly into Yale for a week from September 15th to September 23rd so that I could attend the first two sessions? I would also be happy to meet in Fall 2 in-person when I am back on campus to make up for missing a few of the Fall 1 in-person sessions.

Thanks,
Shaan

My e-mail was met with the following response:

Hi Shaan,

Thanks for your inquiry. Attendance is required for all classes (there are only 5 in total) and there are no makeup assignments. This is a highly interactive course and your participation is needed to contribute to your own and other's learning.

The MGT 432 syllabus is up on classes v2 so you can see when the classes will be held. Also, please note the section on Class Attendance and Participation. Any unapproved absence will result in a deduction of 10% of the final grade. This means for each unexcused absence there is a 10% deduction. In addition, your active participation is 25% of the final grade. So you will need to attend the classes and actively participate in order to not risk failing the course.

Should you need to access any other information, this is a site that students can access: Student Information Systems: http://www.yale.edu/sis/

Best,
Professor XXXXX

To sum up the professor's e-mail, she didn't give a damn about my situation. This was just another example of an authority figure who was inflexible to policy. So what did I do? I stopped asking permission. I flew into Yale for a couple of leadership classes just as I had described in my e-mail and didn't attend the rest because I was working on my business in Las Vegas. I didn't tell my professor. I got an "Honors" for my grade in the class (the second highest grade possible).

At this point, I was pretty annoyed that there were so many people in Yale SOM's administration who were so inflexible to policy. So I decided I was not only going to take my Fall 1 classes remotely, but I was also going to take my Fall 2 classes remotely—just to get an even bigger break to work on my business. And I wasn't going to ask permission to do so.

The only hurdle left to jump was Yale's policy that students are required to take 16 credits each semester. There weren't enough online classes and independent studies for me to get 16 credits remotely from Las Vegas. How would I be able to take 16 credits worth of classes if I was on the other side of the country?

I found a loophole. Yale's policy only requires that students *take* 16 credits worth of classes. Students do not necessarily have to *pass* 16 credits worth of classes. So I could register in a couple of classes at Yale that meet in-person and simply fail them. I would still have enough credits to graduate from the extra classes I had taken previously and would still be playing by the rules—I was in fact still technically enrolled in 16 credits worth of classes!

I learned from my previous mistakes of asking for permission multiple times at Yale. So this time I was going to ask for forgiveness. I didn't e-mail the professors of the two in-person classes I enrolled in at Yale to tell them that I would not be attending lecture or completing any assignments because I'm on the other side of the country. If I had done that, the professors would have been furious. They probably would have exercised their authority to kick me out of the class and alert administration to what I was doing. Instead, I carried out my action without telling them and asked for forgiveness by essentially saying, "Whoops, sorry I didn't do anything for your class!" Sure, my academic transcript now shows that I failed a couple of classes at Yale, but I'm an entrepreneur—so it's not a big deal to me.

My plan worked! I am the first Yale student in history to do an entire MBA semester from 2,500 miles away (without doing a formal study abroad program). I was able to stay in Las Vegas for eight consecutive months to grow my company more rapidly than ever before. And I owe no thanks to asking for permission, but all thanks to asking for forgiveness.

SUCCESS PRACTICE

The next time you would like to get something done that requires approval from an authority, take a step back. Ask yourself, what is the most likely sequence of events that would happen if I ask permission? Then ask, what is the most likely sequence of events that would happen if I carry out my action and ask forgiveness later? If the latter answer is nothing too egregious, then it may be a good choice. After weighing the costs and benefits of each option, you will find that asking for forgiveness rather than permission usually works best.

For people who work in large, bureaucratic organizations, it can be very difficult to use this *Success Strategy*. However, large organizations also don't often have a lot of oversight. No one really noticed that I wasn't on campus at Yale for an entire semester. Similarly, you may be able to take actions that may not typically be acceptable simply because no one will notice. Of course, don't break the law or do anything with serious ethical violations. Always play by the rules—bend them, don't break them.

Success Review

Where in this book did I implicitly mention that I was using the Permission Principle? In *Use the Art of Storytelling*, I talked about how I initially asked over a hundred literary agents and editors to consider my book proposal for an SAT prep book by a perfect-score student. Of course, I was met with over a hundred "No's" to my request.

Now I don't ask for permission when I want to publish a book. I simply publish the book. For example, I did not ask my literary agent for permission to send a book proposal for *Self-Made Success* out to big publishing houses. Instead, I think *Self-Made Success* is a good book idea. So I'm self-publishing it.

Use the Permission Principle—do not ask permission.

CHAPTER 2
WEALTH SUCCESS STRATEGIES

(1) Realize that Million-Dollar Ideas Are Easy
(2) Never Trade Time for Money
(3) Never Expect to Win the Lotto
(4) Be a Big Fish in a Small Pond
(5) Practice Dhandho Philosophy
(6) Capture the Whole Pie

WEALTH SUCCESS STRATEGY #1
REALIZE THAT MILLION-DOLLAR IDEAS ARE EASY

SUCCESS STRATEGY

Million-dollar ideas are everywhere. Having a million-dollar idea is easy. Executing that million-dollar idea is hard.

Execution of million-dollar ideas is difficult because it takes time and effort. Most people don't have the time to pursue the great ideas they have, nor are they willing to put in the effort to bring their ideas to fruition.

Many people are fooled into thinking that what makes million-dollar companies is the idea. The idea doesn't matter all that much. The execution is far more important.

A classic example of people putting too much value on the idea is a TV show I'm very familiar with—*Shark Tank*. *Shark Tank* is so appealing because viewers think to themselves, "Why didn't I think of that?" or "Wow, I could've thought of that simple idea." Viewers are placing way too much importance on the idea of a particular product or service on the show.

What most people don't realize is that the execution by the *Shark Tank* entrepreneurs is far more important. There's often nothing all that special about the ideas that appear on *Shark Tank*. But it's the illusion that ideas are so valuable that can often make the show intoxicatingly addictive to watch. In reality, viewers should be admiring the hustle of the *Shark Tank* entrepreneurs, not the idea itself.

When do most million-dollar ideas come to you? Interestingly, the best ideas often come to me when I am not actively thinking about how to generate a million dollars. I typically have "eureka" moments in the shower, while running, or right before I fall asleep.

The idea for this book actually came to me when I was attempting to fall asleep while I had a horrible fever. Despite having only gotten two hours of sleep the night before and feeling absolutely terrible, my mind just kept racing with ideas for this book. Because I couldn't sleep, I grabbed my iPhone and started writing down different topics to include in this book. Within an hour, I had 80% of the strategies that are now in this book.

Although I'm not sure if *Self-Made Success* will be a million-dollar-book, I certainly consider it one of my better ideas. The only difference between me writing this book and someone else who had an idea for a similar book is that I put in the time and effort to actually execute my idea.

Why do the best ideas often come to us when we least expect it? First, dopamine is released during activities such as showering or exercising. Dopamine can lead our brains to come up with novel ideas. Second, distractions that keep our brain from actively thinking can actually be very beneficial. Our subconscious mind then has a chance to make insightful connections that would be impossible for our conscious mind to make.

I would like to dispel three big myths related to great ideas.

The first myth is that you shouldn't share your big idea with others because they will steal it. This is simply not true. No one believes in your idea as much as you believe in your idea. Because most people will not believe in your idea, they will not put in the time and effort needed to pursue the idea.

The second myth is that the "Big Guy" will crush you. Many people will claim that you shouldn't pursue an idea because a larger company could copy your idea and do it better because they have more resources.

Surprisingly, I actually heard my business partner Mark Cuban say this in an interview with Tai Lopez. Mark said that he didn't think Periscope or Meerkat could succeed because Facebook could start live-streaming and reach a much larger audience. (Note: Periscope and Meerkat are social media applications that allow users to live-stream anything directly from their mobile phones to other users on the application.)

Although I rarely dissent with Mark, I disagree with him here. If every entrepreneur believed a larger company could crush him or her, no companies would ever get started.

You could make the same argument about Mark's own social media application: Cyber Dust -- a mobile chat application that deletes all messages shortly after they are read to maximize privacy. If someone had told Cuban that Cyber Dust would be dust if Facebook Messenger or Apple iMessage implemented a feature that allowed deletion of messages after they are read, would he have still pursued Cyber Dust? My guess is yes.

As an entrepreneur, you have to be overly optimistic and believe that you can do something that no one else can. I'm sure Mark Cuban feels that way about Cyber Dust, and he's probably correct.

In addition, most large companies won't crush you for the same reason that other people won't steal your ideas. No one believes in your idea as much as you believe in your idea. When you are a small startup with virtually no market share, most large companies won't pay attention to you. But if you grow to become a threat to a large company, then they may start paying attention to you. By that time, it's probably too late. You have likely gained too much traction for a large company to kill your business.

A good example of this is Facebook vs. Google. If Mark Zuckerberg had believed the "Big Guy" myth, he would have never started Facebook. During Facebook's early days, an easy way to dismiss the idea would have been to argue that Facebook would be destroyed if Google created its own social media platform. But Google didn't create the platform because they didn't believe in Facebook as much as Mark Zuckerberg believed in Facebook. By the time Google did take notice of Facebook, it was too late. Google tried to create its own social media platform (Google Plus), but Facebook had gained too much traction already. When thinking of million-dollar ideas, don't worry about the "Big Guy."

The third myth related to million-dollar ideas is the "First-Mover" Myth. We have all seen a product or service that is doing remarkably well, and thought, "I had that idea years ago!" Being the first-mover (or at least the first-mover in your mind) on an idea doesn't mean much. It's much more important to be the person who executes the idea best.

For example, I spent the summer of 2012 recording an "on demand" SAT course with one of the world's largest test preparation providers—Veritas Prep. The course consisted of pre-recorded videos of me teaching one hundred strategies to ace the SAT exam. The reason I had to partner with a large test prep company to build this online course was that there weren't many web tools available for me to easily develop an online course on my own (at least, that I knew of at the time).

So I decided that one of the next businesses I wanted to create was a web platform that allowed content producers to easily create and sell online courses. It could be used for SAT courses, yoga courses, accounting courses, cooking courses, etc. Rather than being a content producer myself, I thought there was a much bigger opportunity to create the platform for other content creators.

A couple years later, I learned that companies such as Udemy had been around since 2010 and did exactly what I was thinking of doing. At first, I got angry that I had not pursued my idea earlier. But I now realize that there's no such thing as a "first-mover" advantage on ideas. It's all about who executes the idea the best. In this case, the founders of Udemy (and multiple other online course platforms) put in the time and effort to pursue the idea, and I didn't.

Remember that you can always enter later and do a better job than the "first-mover." For example, I still think the online course platform market can be disrupted (especially since Udemy takes an astronomical fee from instructors that use its platform—50% of revenue). But at this point, I personally can't put in the time and effort necessary to enter this market.

SUCCESS EXAMPLE

For the *Success Example*, I'm going to list five ideas here. I believe all of these are million-dollar ideas. But I have no problem sharing them with everyone because most people will not believe that these are million-dollar ideas. Even if some people do believe that one is a million-dollar idea, they probably won't spend the time and effort necessary to make it come to fruition.

(1) FoodLoop — FoodLoop would be a food discovery app that's essentially "Tinder for Food." But the best part is, the taco can't swipe left. So let's say I can't decide what to eat, but I know I want vegetarian food within a two-mile radius of me that's under $10. I could use the app to quickly swipe through beautiful photos of veggie burgers, cheese enchiladas, falafels, etc. I think pictures are extremely powerful because they don't require the user to read (such as a Yelp review) and they still say a thousand words—one reason why Instagram has gained so much popularity. I also think users want an easy way to fulfill a universal desire—Tinder does this for sex, FoodLoop would do this for food. You could monetize the app through sponsored posts, advertising, and revenue shares of food orders and deliveries.

(2) Karma — Karma would be a positive social network that lets you acknowledge awesome and amazing happenings in the world. The goal is to spread positivity by creating a network that is free from negative and mundane posts. Each user begins the day with seven Karma Points to give friends for great things they are doing. You can give Karma Points because a friend volunteered at a homeless shelter, won a basketball game, bought you a coffee, just graduated college, opened the door for you, etc. You can also select an "Awesome Person of the Day" to acknowledge one of your friends for that day and access "Karma World," which would display the posts that have gotten the most Karma Points on the application. You could monetize the app through sponsored posts and advertising.

(3) Maya — Maya would be a mobile app that allows users to earn and give cash for their posts. For example, once Sarah has posted a photo to Maya, her followers can see the post in their newsfeed, and can click a coin to give $0.01 to the post. Users can keep clicking the coin to give more money to the post. The app would integrate directly with Venmo (a widely used payment application used among millennials) in order to make it easy for users to exchange small amounts of money. The first objection I get to this application is that most users would not want to give money to posts. I agree. But I also think some users would be willing to exchange nominal amounts of cash because it's fun, and I think it's more special to get $0.10 than it is to get ten likes on a post. In addition, some content producers may be able to earn thousands of dollars—e.g., photographers, charities, models, comedians, etc.

You could monetize the app through sponsored posts, advertising, and revenue share.

(4) PhoneClear — PhoneClear would be a device/stand that would be positioned in public places such as airports, movie theaters, malls, and restaurants so that patrons could pay $1 to quickly have their phones cleaned by UV radiation that would kill 99.9% of bacteria on their phones. Most people are not aware that their phones are so dirty (most phones are sixteen times dirtier than a public toilet and 1 in 6 actually has feces on them). To increase awareness of phone uncleanliness, I believe that PhoneClear would need to stir an emotional response in people through a visual mechanism. For example, if people saw just how dirty their phones are under a black light that was attached to the PhoneClear stand, then they may be more likely to purchase a clean.

(5) Passengers on an Airplane — Similar to Humans of New York, Passengers on an Airplane would tell stories of interesting people you meet while sitting next to them on airplanes. Unlike Humans of New York, I would crowd-source the stories and allow anyone to post a photo and story on the Passengers on an Airplane website. Then, I would let users up-vote the most interesting stories. This would result in some great content with lots of social sharing at no cost. You could monetize the website through advertising.

Maybe some of these ideas sound terrible to you. Maybe some of the above ideas already exist. Maybe there is a big player in the market that could crush me if I pursued any of these ideas. Maybe I'm not the first person to have the ideas above. But all of that does not matter as long as these ideas are executed well.

SUCCESS PRACTICE

I don't mind sharing the previous ideas with everyone because I realize that million-dollar ideas are easy to come up with. Begin to take on this mindset of abundance, rather than a mindset of scarcity. It's the first step to wealth.

There is no formula for coming up with million-dollar ideas. As stated previously, most of your best ideas will come to you when you're not actively trying to come up with brilliant ideas. I'm sure you have had at least one million-dollar idea yourself. However, you likely did not pursue it because the execution of the idea was the hard part.

Later in this book, we'll discuss how to vet different ideas, how to use the least resources and money to execute an idea, and how to increase your chances to be successful. But for now, simply realize that million-dollar ideas are easy to come up with … it's the execution that's the hard part.

Success Review

Which previous *Success Strategy* did you notice while I was discussing this one?

Use the Pareto Principle

Notice that I gave you five million-dollar ideas. Given the Pareto Principle that we learned about earlier, how many of those ideas should I pursue? Just one. The 80/20 Principle (or the Pareto Principle) states that 80% of results are due to 20% of effort. Executing just one of these five ideas correctly will likely result in 80% of the revenue that all five ideas would generate combined. The challenge is deciding which idea is the correct one to pursue.

I personally think it is Maya. Although giving money to posts is a wild concept at first, I'm sure that the idea of "liking" posts when it was first introduced was also a wild concept. Before Facebook came out, if someone told me that they are going to post a photo of their family and that I should "like" it as acknowledgement, I would think he or she is a little crazy. Why would I ever "like" a photo?! But that's exactly what we all are accustomed to doing these days. I'm hoping the same will be true for Maya.

Even if Maya doesn't blow up, I think there are so many ways to pivot into the right product-market fit. The most logical pivot that we've thought of so far is pivoting towards charities. Imagine that The Red Cross or United Way could put up posts about specific causes you'd like to support, and with the click of a button you could donate a few cents (or dollars) to a particular cause? Now, it's just time for me and my business school classmate, Vishal Banerjee, to put in the time and effort to make Maya a reality.

WEALTH SUCCESS STRATEGY #2
NEVER TRADE TIME FOR MONEY

SUCCESS STRATEGY

Trading hours for dollars will never lead to significant wealth. You only have 8,760 hours in a year, and much of that is spent sleeping. You must set up revenue streams that continue to produce income even when you sleep.

Passive income is the key to real wealth. Approximately 70% of the world's billionaires started their own businesses. Starting a business is probably the most common way to generate passive income. Of course, it's not easy to start a successful business—50% of small businesses fail within the first five years. That's why I dedicated an entire chapter of this book ("Success Entrepreneurship Strategies") to help you increase your chances of succeeding. But first, let's understand why passive income is so important.

Doctors, lawyers, engineers, and other professionals are essentially highly skilled laborers. Although "laborer" has a negative connotation, I don't mean it as such here. A laborer essentially trades time for money. But there is a ceiling on the money they can earn. That ceiling is the number of hours that they can work.

This is not to say that you should not go to school to have a professional career and start a business instead. The two are not mutually exclusive. I actually think that highly skilled professionals are often the best people to start businesses. To start a successful business, you must first create value. And specific expertise in a particular area can have tremendous value. However, most professionals distribute their value incorrectly—selling value per unit of time. Instead, highly skilled professionals should sell their value per unit of volume by starting a business.

Ironically, I am in school to become a highly skilled laborer—a physician! My ideal career would be to split my time by practicing as a physician four days a week and running my businesses one day a week. However, I don't think that my salary as a doctor will come close to the money generated from the businesses I own. Why practice as a physician then? Because I believe there's something liberating about helping patients without having to worry about my paycheck.

The good news about generating a passive income stream is that it is easier than ever because of the Internet. Fifty years ago, creating a passive income stream was difficult. To build a business, you'd have to invest in infrastructure and were limited by location and hours. Now, the Internet makes it virtually costless to open a store that's open 24 hours to a customer base of 7.5 billion. Scalability through the Internet has made it easier than ever to avoid trading time for money.

SUCCESS EXAMPLE

My father is the perfect example of a highly skilled professional who amassed wealth without trading hours for dollars. My dad and my mom came to the United States from India in the 1980's with $65 in their pockets. My dad went to pharmacy school in India, but was unable to practice as a pharmacist in Chicago where they originally lived because of a state licensing issue. My parents worked odd jobs, including in fast food restaurants, to make ends meet. When my dad found out that he could practice as a pharmacist in Nevada, my parents moved to Las Vegas. That's where I was born.

After practicing as a pharmacist for some time, my parents were ready to move out of the small apartment we had been living in to a house. But that's when my dad got some good advice from a family friend who owned a motel. He told my dad not to buy house, but a motel instead. A house would continue to drain my dad's income, but a motel would allow my dad to generate income passively. So my dad bought the motel next to this family friend instead of buying a house, and that's where I grew up for the first sixteen years of my life. It wasn't a pretty motel, but it helped my dad generate passive income while he was at work as a pharmacist.

After living in the motel for a few years, the owners of the gas station just down the street wanted to sell their business. So my dad bought it too. My dad split his time between practicing as a pharmacist, running a motel, and operating a gas station. But most of his income was not from his primary profession as a pharmacist. Instead, it was from the passive income streams he had created for himself through the motel and gas station.

From growing up in a small village in India to now living in his 8,000 square-foot dream home, my dad is the embodiment of the American dream.

Success Practice

I want to give you some ideas about how you can generate a passive income stream. Here are three that work for me.

(1) Write A Book — I'm creating a new passive income stream right now by writing this book! It's easier than ever to write a book. I would recommend self-publishing your e-book through Amazon Kindle Direct Publishing and print book through CreateSpace as I have done for *Self-Made Success*. Even if your book does not make you an astronomical amount in royalties, you will be seen as an expert in whatever field you choose to write about. Of course, make sure that you are actually an expert on the topic that you write about and that you are providing massive value to your readers.

(2) Create Videos — My SAT prep videos on YouTube have gotten millions of views, resulting in thousands of dollars in royalties. I'm sure that you can develop videos that are more entertaining than my SAT prep videos. If you think writing a book is too boring, create entertaining videos for YouTube. You will create a passive income stream that may eventually become greater than your primary income stream.

(3) Develop An Online Course — Are you an expert in a particular field? Of course you are. Everyone has a talent. And if you don't have specialized knowledge of a particular discipline, start developing it. Read, learn, and practice everything you can related to a particular topic. Then, create an online course teaching others about it. This is what I did with my knowledge of the SAT. I developed an SAT prep course teaching others how to prepare for the SAT the way that I did in high school. I knew more about it than anyone else because I spent thousands of hours preparing myself and writing prep material for the SAT. By far, my SAT course is my greatest passive income stream.

Success Review

Which previous *Success Strategy* did you notice while I was discussing this one?

Use the Pareto Principle

Notice that I said that I would like to practice as a physician four days a week and work on my businesses one day a week. Given the Pareto Principle, what percent of my total income will my businesses likely generate? 80%.

Although I would dedicate more time to practicing as a physician, I still anticipate my businesses to generate more income for me overall. In other words, 20% of my time will generate 80% of my income. That's why you should never trade time for money.

Wealth Success Strategy #3
Never Expect to Win the Lotto

Success Strategy

On your path to accumulating wealth, never expect it to happen overnight. This is a sobering reality for most people, especially millennials.

The lotto is such an interesting social phenomenon. People are attracted by the idea of instant wealth without effort. In addition, people become more attracted to the lotto as the prize grows, even though their chances of winning diminishes greatly.

Similar to the lotto, the bigger the market that you enter in business, the lower your chances of succeeding, because there is more competition. Unlike the lotto, instant millionaires are not born in business.

Today, the appeal of overnight millionaires is more enticing than ever. Social media provides instant gratification. You put a photo up, and it immediately gets likes. But if you put a product out, you will not immediately receive cash. On social media, you may see a video go viral that causes an unknown person to become an instant success. But you should treat these viral successes like the lotto—an unrealistic possibility.

I remember being a young, naive entrepreneur who was first starting Prep Expert in college. I thought I would be an overnight success with hundreds of students immediately enrolling in my SAT prep classes. Boy did reality slap me in the face! I barely got enough students to enroll in my first set of classes. But there was a silver lining. After I produced value for the first set of students (a 376-point average score improvement), the next set of classes became easier to enroll, then the next one, then the next one, etc.

You can surely be a success. But you will surely not be an overnight success. Patience is a virtue. You must be willing to put in the effort necessary to grind it out through the tough times, especially in the beginning when most people would quit. You likely have a winning idea, you just don't know it yet. Stop wishing to win the lotto with your idea and start putting in more time and effort than anyone else around you—it will pay off.

Success Example

There is a reason that Albert Einstein called compound interest "the most powerful force in the universe." It can certainly generate great wealth. But the key is that the wealth accumulates slowly. Here is an example adapted from JP Morgan Asset Management.

Assume that each of the three people below puts $5,000 into an investment account that generates 7% annual return.

> **Person 1** — Invests $5,000 annually between 25 and 35. By the time she is 65, she will have $602,070.
>
> **Person 2** — Invests $5,000 annually between 35 and 65. By the time she is 65, she will have $540,741.
>
> **Person 3** — Invests $5,000 annually between 25 and 65. By the time she is 65, she will have $1,142,811.

Notice how slow and steady ... and EARLY wins the race. Can you believe that Person 1 accumulated more money even though she invested $100,000 less than Person 2? All because she had the patience to make her investment earlier. Of course, Person 3 is the real winner here because she not only started early, but stayed with it the whole time.

Compound interest is powerful, but you must have the patience to wait it out. I'm not saying you have to wait forty years for a payout on your effort, but accumulating wealth requires patience.

Success Review

Which previous *Success Strategy* did you notice while I was discussing this one?

Realize that Million-Dollar Ideas Are Easy

Notice that I said, "You likely have a winning idea, you just don't know it yet." This goes back to our previous concept that ideas are easy, but execution is difficult. Even when you have a million-dollar idea, it may take years before it manifests. Have patience and never expect to win the lotto.

Success Wealth Strategy #4
Be a Big Fish in a Small Pond

Success Strategy

One surefire way to increase your chances of monetary success is to be a big fish in a small pond. Essentially, it's better to enter a small market with less competition than it is to enter a large market with many incumbent players.

This strategy mainly refers to cities. You have a higher chance of success in a smaller city than a larger one. However, this strategy can also apply to the Internet. The Internet is the largest market with the most competition. Therefore, you need to carve out a niche for yourself on the Internet with less competition—at least to start.

This strategy not only works well for business, but also for highly skilled professionals. Doctors and lawyers in smaller cities often earn higher salaries and gain greater recognition than their counterparts in larger cities. With fewer options to the population in small cities, highly skilled professionals can act as monopolists. I remember having a conversation with a very wealthy lawyer in Las Vegas. He mentioned that it was much easier for him to find success in Las Vegas than it was for him to have success in Washington DC where lawyers are a dime a dozen.

This strategy also applies to academics. It's much more advantageous to go to a school in a city that is known for poor academics than it so to attend a school in a city that is known for stellar academics. Your opportunity to stand out as a top student is much greater in the former.

For example, it was a blessing for me to attend inner-city public schools in Las Vegas, which are known for having practically the worst academics in the nation with a 40% dropout rate. It was much easier for me to become my high school valedictorian. It was much easier to win scholarships that were only open to Nevada students from companies such as Coca-Cola, Toyota, and McDonald's. It was much easier to get into great colleges such as Brown, Northwestern, and Johns Hopkins (because colleges need students from every geographic region). I'm not sure I would have had the same levels of academic success had I attended an ultra-competitive high school in San Jose.

Success Example

When I was first starting Prep Expert, I was a senior in college at USC. My plan was to advertise the classes on my website during the spring and teach classes during the summer, before I headed to medical school. I had to decide where I wanted to start my Prep Expert classes.

I thought it made perfect sense to start my classes in Los Angeles. Because Los Angeles is a huge market with a lot of wealth, I just had to convince a dozen parents to enroll in my SAT prep classes. Easy right? Wrong.

I tried everything to launch Prep Expert. I paid the deposit to rent a beautiful, modern classroom near Beverly Hills to advertise on our website. I e-mailed every college counselor in the Los Angeles area about our classes. I visited over 50 top high schools in the Los Angeles area. I did web and print advertising. But I could not get one student enrolled in our classes.

Right before spring break, I had a student from my high school in Las Vegas e-mail me. He said that he wanted to take my classes, and was hoping that I'd start them in Las Vegas. No one but me knew at the time that I had zero students in Los Angeles and one potential student in Las Vegas. So I pivoted. I cancelled my deposit on the Los Angeles classroom and made a new deposit on a Las Vegas classroom.

Prep Expert was now going to launch in Las Vegas, rather than Los Angeles. I told the Las Vegas student, and he enrolled. I now had my first student in Las Vegas without doing any marketing there.

The difference between starting my business in Las Vegas versus Los Angeles was night and day. In Los Angeles, I didn't have one student enroll for months. In Las Vegas, I had students enroll weekly. By the time June came around for me to teach the first set of Prep Expert SAT classes, I had not one, but two classes that were almost completely full in Las Vegas.

I'm fairly certain that I didn't succeed in Los Angeles because there is so much competition there for SAT prep. Test prep companies have been there for dozens of years with deep customer bases. So it was very hard for a solo entrepreneur like myself to enter the market. But Las Vegas did not have many test prep options. So it was much easier to start there. We are now the largest test prep provider in Las Vegas.

Moral of the story? Be a big fish in a small pond.

Success Practice

For entrepreneurs, consider setting up shop in a small city, not a large one. Your business will likely do much better in an environment where you are not surrounded by cutthroat competition. A bigger market does not always equal greater revenue.

For highly skilled professionals, consider living in a small city, not a large one. You will not only likely earn a higher salary, but you will also garner greater recognition than you would have in a large city. Just because you're a lawyer doesn't mean you have to live in New York or Washington, DC. In fact, it may be advantageous for you not to.

For parents and students, rethink moving to a city with the best academics. I personally know many families who moved out of Las Vegas because of the poor school system. Then, their children suffered in some of the most competitive academic environments around the nation. Little did they know that the "poor" Vegas school system could have been one of their child's biggest advantages.

SUCCESS REVIEW

Which previous *Success Strategy* did you notice while I was discussing this one?

Never Expect to Win the Lotto

Believing that it's better to enter a larger market because there are more dollars is like attempting to win the lottery. Your eyes are fixed on the big prize. This is likely why investors hate when entrepreneurs describe how big their market is (e.g., $100 billion) and then say that they only need to capture 1% of that. The bigger the market, the harder it is to capture any market share at all. For an immediate advantage, be a big fish in a small pond.

Wealth Success Strategy #5
Practice Dhandho Philosophy

Success Strategy

"Dhandho" is a Gujarati word that means "endeavors that create wealth." To Practice Dhandho Philosophy means to take low-risk, high-reward approaches to business, investment, saving, and spending.

I first formally learned about Dhandho Philosophy when a friend told me that I should read Mohnish Pabrai's *The Dhandho Investor*. While the book is primarily about value investing, Pabrai also describes the group of people that have used the Dhandho Philosophy most effectively: Patel motel-owners. With little education or capital, Patels immigrated to the United States in the late twentieth century and began applying the Dhandho Philosophy to business. They now own over $40 billion in hospitality-associated assets in the USA and employ over a million people.

I have been immersed in Dhandho Philosophy my entire life, but just never knew what it was called. It has been deeply ingrained in the culture of Gujaratis. As a child, I used to think my parents were just being "cheap." For example, my mom would never allow me to get a soda from Taco Bell because we had soda at home. Although taking frugality to this level might sound ridiculous, this practice of saving is part of larger Dhandho Philosophy that has led to massive wealth for many Indian Americans. According to the U.S. Census

Bureau, Indian Americans are in fact the wealthiest ethnic group in America.

Of course, the above is an example of applying Dhandho Philosophy to personal spending. However, the power of Dhandho Philosophy increases exponentially when it is applied to business. In fact, Mark Cuban definitely Practices Dhandho Philosophy. Marks' famous for saying, "Only morons start a business on a loan." Essentially, do not start something as high-risk as a new business with something as high-risk as a loan.

In addition, Mark chose to go to Indiana University because it had the least expensive tuition. Similarly, I chose to go to USC because they gave me a full-tuition scholarship. Mark used to sleep on the floor in college and have a closet as his room. I currently choose to take the smallest room in our three-bedroom apartment at Yale so that I would only have to spend $500/month on rent—that's just $6,000 a year for housing! Of course, you need to balance frugality with enjoying life. But most people do way too much of the latter and not enough of the former.

There are only two ways to become wealthy: make more money or spend less money. Doing both of these together can have exponentially powerful effects. To make more money, build value to create passive income streams. To spend less money, practice Dhandho Philosophy in all aspects of your life.

Success Example

Let's go over a practical example of how I applied the Dhandho Philosophy to business. When I first wanted to start Prep Expert in college, I ran into a chicken and egg problem. I needed to have a location to run classes to advertise on the website, but I didn't want to lease a location until I had a few student enrollments to cover my costs of leasing a location.

What do you think most people would have done in my situation? They might take out a business loan to secure a short-term lease on a retail location, rent temporary furniture such as classroom desks, and hire a receptionist to staff the location in case parents wanted to drop in.

But I was a college student who had $900 left over from my scholarships to start this business. And I've never taken a loan in my life, and I wasn't about to take one to start my business. So I channeled my Indian immigrant heritage's Dhandho Philosophy and found another way.

I came across executive office co-working spaces. These locations typically have conference rooms that seat ten to fifteen people, which are equipped with whiteboards and large LCD TVs. In addition, they have receptionists staffed at the location during business hours to help any parents that may drop in to look at the location.

The best part was that I could rent the conference room only for the hours that I needed it. This meant that I would not have the overhead costs of leasing, furnishing, and staffing my own location. Applying Dhandho Philosophy allowed me to save thousands of dollars that other test prep companies waste.

Success Practice

For business, Practice Dhandho Philosophy by finding alternatives to loans to fund your idea. Most Internet businesses can be started for little to no capital because of the plethora of free and cheap web tools available. If your business does require a significant amount of capital to start, try saving enough money from your current job, finding new jobs to generate enough income to fund your idea, starting a crowd-funding campaign, or considering a less capital-intensive business altogether.

For personal savings, stop wasteful spending. This is a simple way to Practice Dhandho Philosophy. As Benajmin Franklin said, "A penny saved is a penny earned." Figure out a way to save $5 to $10 a day. By the end of the week, deposit your extra cash into your bank account. It may not seem like a lot at first, but over time, your bank account will grow exponentially. This is not really due to the little bit of money that you are saving, but more so due to the Dhandho Philosophy eventually becoming ingrained in all aspects of your life.

SUCCESS REVIEW

Which previous *Success Strategy* did you notice while I was discussing this one?

Never Expect to Win the Lotto

Practicing Dhandho Philosophy will not make you an overnight millionaire. That's like expecting to win the lotto. Although many Patel motel owners are millionaires, it did not happen immediately. They often put in decades of hard work with discriminate spending and investing. Practicing Dhandho Philosophy will make you rich, but you have to be disciplined about it.

Which other previous *Success Strategy* did you notice while I was discussing this one?

Never Trade Time for Money

I mentioned that you can magnify the power of the Dhandho Philosophy by combining it with passive income streams. Many

Patel motel owners, like my dad, did this. They had full-time jobs, but also owned motels to create passive income streams.

Be careful when using this *Success Strategy*. I have seen too many people take the Dhandho Philosophy to the extreme. For example, some people spend hours driving around only to save a few dollars. You have to remember that time is more valuable than money. As *Shark Tank* star Daymond John says, "Time is the only luxury." Use the *Success Strategies* Never Trade Time for Money and Practice Dhandho Philosophy together to create the ultimate combination for wealth creation.

Wealth Success Strategy #6
Capture the Whole Pie

Success Strategy

Barry Nalebuff, my professor at Yale and co-founder of Honest Tea, would say, "Let's think of all revenue generated as a pie." It's your job to capture as much of that pie as possible.

As you generate more revenue, you will become a target. People will take notice of your increasing income. You will have all kinds of people who will promise to make you even richer.

While some people may have good intentions, most people just see deep pockets. It's your job to separate the people and businesses that can actually increase your ROI from those that are just looking to take a bigger slice out of your pie. It can be extremely difficult to tell the difference between the two.

In addition, you need to re-examine how the revenue you generate is being split. Are you capturing the majority of the pie? Is there a service-provider that is taking too much of your revenue? Are there unnecessary fees?

Capturing the whole pie means to avoid giving up too much of the value you created to others.

SUCCESS EXAMPLE

When I was in college, it was my dream to author an SAT prep book to help other students prepare for the SAT the way that I did in high school. I read a book about how to publish a nonfiction book. The first step was to write a book proposal to send out to literary agents. If a literary agent chooses to represent you, he or she will then send your book proposal to contacts in the publishing industry. If an acquisitions editor likes your book proposal, he or she will offer you a book deal so that you can earn royalties.

The chances of a first-time, unknown author like myself of getting a book deal are slim to none. After getting over a hundred rejections from literary agents and publishing houses, you can imagine how ecstatic I was when McGraw-Hill, the world's largest education publisher, finally offered me a book deal (although they initially rejected my book proposal, until they saw what I was building with Prep Expert). I thought I had made it! Not only would I be a published author at 22 years old, but I would also have the marketing prowess of one of the world's largest book publishers.

My McGraw-Hill book *SAT 2400 In Just 7 Steps* was published in July of 2012. However, it was not as expected. McGraw-Hill did not do much for the marketing of my book. Although the distribution of the book into Barnes & Noble and public libraries was certainly a plus, I had to evaluate whether it was worth all that I was giving up to McGraw-Hill. So let's calculate it. (Note that this is also the industry standard.)

McGraw-Hill offered me 10% of net sales on the book. McGraw-Hill sold my book to Amazon and Barnes & Noble for $8 apiece. This meant that I get $0.80 per book sold. In addition, my literary agent took a 15% commission off of that. So I'm left with $0.64 for a book that I put over a thousand hours of blood, sweat, and tears into writing.

Let's look at the whole pie. The book retailed for $16 and approximately 40,000 copies have now been sold. This means that I would receive approximately $27,200 out of a total pie of $640,000. I love McGraw-Hill for giving me a chance as a first-time author, but it was time for me to capture the whole pie.

For my next SAT books, I went the self-publishing route. This allowed me to capture 70% of the retail $9.99 price that they sell for. You might argue that my distribution would decrease without a big publisher like McGraw-Hill. While that might be true, how many books would I need to sell to make $27,000? Less than 4,000 copies. So even if my New SAT book sales decreased by 90%, I would still make the same amount in royalties going the self-publishing route as I would have with a big publisher.

In today's world that operates on the Internet, I believe large publishing houses will eventually become extinct. They don't provide enough value to an author to capture 90% of the author's pie. The Internet can connect authors directly with their readers. Why have a middleman?

I don't think this is just true for book publishers. There are so many industries with middlemen with high fees that are undeserved. Look at your own life and determine how you can reorganize to capture the whole pie.

Success Practice

I try to avoid recurring subscription fees as much as possible. These services are great to offer if you own a business because people either don't use your services nearly as much as they initially thought (e.g., gym memberships) or sometimes forget that they are subscribed at all.

But subscription services are often terrible for the consumer. Think of your income as the pie. How much of your pie is going to subscription services? How could you reduce the amount of your pie that is being eaten by subscription services? One way would be to discontinue the subscription service altogether. But some subscription services are worth it (e.g., Netflix).

Another way would be to spread the loss of your pie around. Here's a practical way that you can do it if you are an iPhone user.

Music is expensive. And music piracy is illegal, unethical, and so 20th century. To solve this problem, Apple, Spotify, and TIDAL started subscription-based streaming services. Apple Music charges an individual $9.99 per month for unlimited streaming. One hundred and twenty dollars per year for unlimited legal music isn't bad. But let's reduce how much of our income pie Apple captures by spreading it around. An Apple Music Family Plan is $14.99 per month for unlimited streaming and allows up to six users. By sharing an Apple Music Family Plan with six of your family members or friends, you have effectively reduced your cost of Apple Music to $2.50 per month or $30 per year.

Capturing the whole pie means reducing the size of the slices that undeserving outside parties are eating. Think of more ways you can do this in both your business and your personal life.

Success Review

Which previous *Success Strategy* did you notice while I was discussing this one?

Practice Dhandho Philosophy

Notice how I refused to let McGraw-Hill take 90% of the value I created. Instead, I found a way to give my new book distributor and publisher, Amazon, just 30% of the value I created. Finding ways to save as much as possible, especially when the result is virtually identical, is all part of the Dhandho Philosophy.

CHAPTER 3
ENTREPRENEURSHIP SUCCESS STRATEGIES

(1) Do What You Know
(2) Start a Service-Based Company
(3) Develop an Unreasonable Obsession
(4) Just Launch
(5) Never Go to a Gunfight Without Bullets
(6) Realize Bureaucracy Is the Root of All Evil

Entrepreneurship Success Strategy #1
Do What You Know

Success Strategy

Billionaire Warren Buffet has said that he is a successful investor because he stays within the realms of what he knows. This could not be more true for entrepreneurs. The first rule of entrepreneurship is to Do What You Know.

When I was a junior in college, I attended a speaking event with Timothy Ferris, the author of *The 4-Hour Workweek*. One of the attendees asked Ferris what kind of business the audience should think about starting. Ferris responded with, "Do something you have expertise in." He said that he knew a lot about bodybuilding, so he started a sports nutrition company. I remember being completely unsatisfied with this answer. I wanted Ferris to tell us *exactly* what kind of business we should start. He was the author of *The 4-Hour Workweek*. Shouldn't he have the secret to success? It wasn't until years later that I realized he did give us the secret to success.

One of the biggest mistakes I see entrepreneurs make is attempting to enter an industry that they are not familiar with. If you have no knowledge of an industry, you are shooting yourself in the foot before you even start the race. But if you have deep knowledge of a particular topic, you immediately have a competitive advantage.

The second biggest mistake I see entrepreneurs make is not building massive value in the industry they plan to enter. There is no such thing as a get-rich-quick scheme. Most people are not willing to put in the time and effort necessary to build massive value.

Malcolm Gladwell's 10,000-hour rule from his famous book *Outliers* posits that it takes 10,000 hours of practice in order to become a master at anything—sports, music, academics, etc. The same is true for business. Although it may not take 10,000 hours to build massive value, it will certainly take a significant amount of time and effort.

SUCCESS EXAMPLE

In college when I was thinking of starting a business, I had to ask myself, "What is something I know how to do really well?" The answer to that question was, "Not much." There weren't a lot of things that I knew extraordinarily well. But there was one thing: the SAT.

I got a perfect score on the SAT and I could leverage that. In addition, what was special about my perfect SAT score is that I didn't start out with a very high SAT score—I was just barely above average. I then spent 1,000 hours (not 10,000 hours) preparing for the SAT. And it paid off with college acceptances, scholarships, and academic awards.

I was now willing to put in another thousand hours to build massive value for other students—to develop curriculum to help other students prepare exactly as I did in high school. This is the part that most entrepreneurs would skip. Many people would have been inclined to just use books from other companies because they don't want to put in the effort themselves.

The willingness to put in an incredible amount of sweat equity to build massive value is what separates successful entrepreneurs from unsuccessful entrepreneurs. Not only should you do what you know, but you should also build massive value in what you know in order to have highest likelihood of succeeding as an entrepreneur.

SUCCESS PRACTICE

You might be thinking, "I don't know anything that well!" Don't worry, I thought the same thing when I was first starting out. So let's do an exercise to help you think of some ideas. Answer the following three questions:

(1) What topics would you consider yourself an expert at?
(2) What is something you have worked extremely hard at in your life?
(3) What are some of your greatest accomplishments?

Hopefully you now have some ideas. The ideal situation would be if there was one theme that showed up as an answer to all three questions. If that happened, you now know in what industry you should start a business.

Once you have a particular topic identified, answer the following three questions:

(1) Can you write a book, create informational videos, or create an online course about your topic?
(2) How could you make your book, videos, or online course different than what's already out there?
(3) How could you disrupt the industry as it currently stands?

With this simple brainstorming session, you likely have many ideas for a business that you might want to start. Guess what? Your idea is probably a winner. Now, it's time to put in your "10,000" hours to make it a reality.

If you weren't able to come up with some areas of expertise that you have, then you need to become an expert. To become an expert, choose a topic or discipline that really interests you. Ideally, pick a topic in an industry in which people are regularly spending money (health, education, food, beauty, etc.). Now, spend a thousand hours learning everything you can about that topic. That's just step one. Then, spend a thousand hours building massive value for your future customers.

Success Review

Which previous *Success Strategy* did you notice while I was discussing this one?

Realize that Million-Dollar Ideas Are Easy

Notice that I didn't have a really complex formula for how to find your next business idea. As we learned before, million-dollar ideas are everywhere. But this strategy took us one step further and clarified that people who have deep knowledge are typically best positioned to execute million-dollar ideas. Execution is once again more important than the idea itself. Put in thousands of hours building massive value in the realm of what you know to have the best chance of bringing your million-dollar idea to fruition.

Entrepreneurship Success Strategy #2
Start a Service-Based Company

Success Strategy

Should you create a product or a service? The answer is simple—a service. Products are dead. Starting a service-based business is much less capital-intensive and has a higher probability of success than a product-based business for the solopreneur.

When you think of an innovative entrepreneur, you typically think of an inventor who tinkers with materials to develop a new product. In fact, most people are surprised to hear that I went on *Shark Tank* because I haven't invented a product. I want you to reimagine your image of an innovative entrepreneur as someone who produces massive value by providing a service. In fact, with every new season of *Shark Tank*, more and more service-based companies and apps are appearing on the show.

Technology companies used to sell software as a product. They now sell it as a service. In recent years, the trend in the software industry has been to sell SAS, or Software As a Service. This way, software is paid for on a monthly or subscription basis rather than as a one-time purchase. This not only increases the profits of software companies, but it also helps reduce the piracy of their services.

But whether you are creating an online service or an in-person service (or both), your strategy when creating a service-based business should remain the same. First, your service needs to be unbelievably effective and deliver results, preferably measurable results. Second, you want to de-commoditize your service. If your service is just a commodity—something that is easily interchangeable—then it will be difficult to turn a profit, especially if there is fierce competition.

Success Example

One of the reasons Prep Expert has been profitable is because it is a service. It started out as an in-person SAT prep class in Las Vegas, as a service. Then it expanded into private tutoring, as a service. Then it expanded into an online SAT prep class, as a service. Then it expanded into online weekend SAT and ACT prep camps, as a service. Then it expanded into in-person SAT prep classes in twenty cities, as a service. Then it expanded into online and in-person ACT prep classes, as a service. Then it expanded into college admissions consulting, as a service. Now, it's expanded into online and in-person Self-Made Success courses, as a service.

And I'm excited to see what Prep Expert expands into next. That is the beauty of a service. You might start small, but then you have all kinds of opportunities to expand it into new areas and scale it with the Internet. For products, it takes a lot of research, development, and capital to develop your next product to expand your product line.

Of course, developing a service is not easy. It does take thousands of hours of work to build a really awesome service. But it's usually a lot cheaper to create a service. In addition, for regular solo entrepreneurs, a service is something they can work on by themselves without having to rely on engineers, designers, or factories to build their product.

Prep Expert has been successful for the two reasons I mentioned before. First, it delivers unbelievably effective, measurable results.

After a six-week SAT prep course, the average SAT score improvement in our classes has been 368 points—the equivalent of jumping from the 50th percentile to the 90th percentile on the SAT.

Second, I have de-commoditized the service by embedding my personal story directly into the curriculum. While other test-prep services may try to copy our strategies, they can't copy me. You simply can't get an online course with me (or one of my hand-picked instructors whom I train) teaching my SAT prep material with as much passion and insight anywhere else.

SUCCESS PRACTICE

When thinking about starting a service-based company, you need to think about user experience. Most people think of user experience as the way in which a user interacts with a piece of software or a mobile app. But there is a user experience to everything. There is a user experience when you go to McDonald's to order a hamburger. There is also a (much better) user experience when you go to the Apple Store to buy an iPhone.

When you create a service-based company, you need to think about how to make the customer user experience as amazing as possible. For example, at Prep Expert, I thought students would have a better user experience if we gave them an Amazon Kindle tablet to read all of our SAT e-books on. This way, they don't have to carry around heavy SAT books everywhere. As an added bonus, high school students like it that they just got a free tablet by enrolling in our in-person courses! Always think about user experience and how to improve it in your service-based company.

You also need to think about how to scale your service-based company. The easiest way to do so is online. There are so many web tools available to help you reach a wider audience. If you are creating a pre-recorded online course to sell, consider Thinkific as a potential platform. If you are delivering content in a live online format (whether it's a course or consulting), consider ClickMeeting as a potential platform. There are a number of other resources. Find which one you like best to start scaling your service-based business using the Internet.

Success Review

Which previous *Success Strategy* did you notice while I was discussing this one?

Practice Dhandho Philosophy

Starting a service-based business is usually not capital-intensive, but can be highly profitable. This follows the low-risk, high-reward precept of the Dhandho Philosophy. You may argue that Patels who practiced Dhandho Philosophy opened a capital-intensive business: motels. However, this business is a service, not a product. The Patels who immigrated to the United States in the 1970's and 1980's also didn't have a choice—the Internet was not an option. There will be a new wave of entrepreneurs who practice Dhandho Philosophy to start Internet-based service companies to generate massive wealth—will you be one?

Entrepreneurship Success Strategy #3
Develop an Unreasonable Obsession

Success Strategy

The lone entrepreneur needs to be obsessed with the objective. In order to succeed, you must think about your business all day, every day.

Obsession is different than passion. Obsession is a preoccupation, whereas passion is excitement. You don't need to be passionate about what you are creating, but you do need to be obsessed with creating it. For example, I am not passionate about SAT prep material, but I am obsessed with developing the best SAT prep material on this planet.

Developing an obsession is important because as an entrepreneur you have to be the hardest working person in the room. Mark Cuban often says, "Work like there's someone working twenty-four hours a day to take it all away from you." His *Shark Tank* co-star Lori Greiner says, "Entrepreneurs are willing to work 80 hours a week to avoid working 40 hours a week." In order to work so hard, you will need to be obsessed with what you are creating. If you are not obsessed, burnout is inevitable.

Business school can actually make people hesitant to become entrepreneurs. The problem with business school is that it attempts to turn entrepreneurship into a science. But entrepreneurship is not a science; it is an art. If you listen to your economics professor, you would think there would be no way to start a successful business because you would get crushed by incumbent competition and all profits would eventually equal marginal cost.

But sometimes it's better to ignore logic and reason, and follow your obsession. The successful entrepreneur has to be a naive, wide-eyed, optimistic maverick who believes he or she can do what no one else can—succeed against all odds.

Success Example

When I was starting Prep Expert in college, I was absolutely obsessed with making it work. I would think about creating Prep Expert in class, I would think about creating Prep Expert on vacation, I would think about creating Prep Expert at the gym, I would think about creating Prep Expert while I was eating. I was obsessed with Prep Expert all day, every day.

I remember doing HIIT (High Intensity Interval Training) on the treadmill at the gym and all I was thinking about was Prep Expert. The next thing you know, my phone starts getting a call from Grace Freedson—the most prominent literary agent in the test prep industry. I had called Grace the day before and left her a message about how I was seeking representation for an SAT prep book I was working on. I had already been rejected by over one hundred literary agents, and I was rather certain that she would not be interested either. But I jumped off the treadmill to pick up the phone to see what she had to say. She was definitely interested. I was huffing and puffing on the phone since I was running at twelve miles per hour on the treadmill, but I didn't care—I was obsessed with making my dream a reality. Grace later went on to help me secure a book deal with McGraw-Hill.

I remember skipping many social events because I was obsessed with developing Prep Expert. And I had no problem doing so because I was obsessed with building my business. In fact, I remember e-mailing proposals for an online course partnership to many major test prep companies on New Year's Eve. I did not care that I was not out with the rest of the world celebrating the New Year because I was obsessed with making sure I landed a partnership. One of those e-mails helped me land a partnership with Veritas Prep, in which we developed an online course that generated millions of dollars in revenue!

Success Practice

To develop an obsession, I would not suggest listing your passions. As stated previously, there is a nuanced difference between an obsession and a passion. Of course, it is possible to be both passionate and obsessed with the same objective.

Instead, decide what you can do better than anyone else on this planet. If you really believe you have the knowledge, tools, and expertise to do something ten times better than the next guy, then you will likely develop an obsession to prove that.

Developing an unreasonable obsession might make others think you are crazy. You'll have to walk the fine line between crazy and genius. When you are just starting your business, everyone will think that you are the former. But when you succeed, everyone will think you are the latter.

Success Review

Which previous *Success Strategy* did you notice while I was discussing this one?

Use the Law of Attraction

Notice the following lines: "I would think about creating Prep Expert in class, I would think about creating Prep Expert on vacation, I would think about creating Prep Expert at the gym, I would think about creating Prep Expert while I was eating. I was obsessed with Prep Expert all day, every day."

Although I didn't know it at the time, I was using the Law of Attraction to start my business. The first step to using the Law of Attraction is to think about your desires. The next step is to feel like your vision is already a reality. I certainly did that with Prep Expert. Developing an unreasonable obsession and using the Law of Attraction go hand-in-hand.

ENTREPRENEURSHIP SUCCESS STRATEGY #4
JUST LAUNCH

SUCCESS STRATEGY

Entrepreneurs have too much trepidation about having the perfect launch strategy for their product or service. Stop being so precise. Just release your service and iterate as you go.

In addition to deterring students from wanting to create a business, business school also causes students to overanalyze before they launch their entrepreneurial venture. I have seen too many people worry way too much about customer feedback, market research, and competitive forces before they have even released their product or service. It gets so bad that they stagnate, freeze up, delay the release, or don't launch at all.

I've read *The Lean Start-Up* by Eric Ries and understand minimum viable products, product-market fit, rapid iteration, listening to customers, etc. This is also all that's talked about in entrepreneurship classes, seminars, and conferences. Trust me, I've been to enough of them to know. But the problem with the lean start-up method is that it's easy to get bogged down in all of the feedback. You make the mistake of trying to be everything to everyone. But you can't, and won't, please everyone.

I believe more in the Steve Jobs approach: people don't know what they want. If Steve Jobs had asked for customer feedback about flip phones in 2003, do you think any customer would have asked for a mobile device that you can interact with completely with touch?

Probably not, and the iPhone would have never been created. Henry Ford is also famous for saying, "If I had asked people what they wanted, they would have said faster horses." And the Ford automobile would have never been created.

So how can you reduce the risk of creating a product or service that people will not use if you are not going to spend all day getting customer feedback? Create a product or service that you yourself would use and pay for. If you are the customer for your product or service, you have all the feedback you need to launch. Build something that you yourself would love, rather than trying to build something that some person you know nothing about would hypothetically love because you have a guess that they will.

Finally, ignore the competition. Many entrepreneurs do way too much research into the competition. Once you understand some basic points about your competition such as core competencies, service offerings, and price points, move on. Focus on building your own business, not following someone else's.

Success Example

When I started Prep Expert, I did not ask one student whether they liked my strategies before I released my book and course. Instead, I simply developed one hundred SAT prep strategies that I thought would help students.

I did not look at the competition's price points for their courses. Instead, I simply priced it at $999 for a 60-hour course because I thought $17 per hour was a fair price to pay.

I did not ask students how long they thought the course should be. Instead, I simply made it sixty hours because I thought ten hours per week for six weeks was necessary for significant score improvements.

In addition, I launched my website for Prep Expert and started selling the course before I had even written half of my book or developed any curriculum. I just launched.

And it worked. Now I might seem a bit arrogant for doing all these things without asking anyone else's permission. But there's a reason my strategy still worked: I built a service that I myself would use and was an expert at.

Because I had vast experience in preparing for the SAT, I knew what my students needed better than they knew what they needed. Of course, I have iterated the curriculum of my class multiple times to make it even better since the pilot course.

But just because it wasn't perfect at first didn't scare me away from launching altogether. It was certainly good at first, but I now believe it's great. You need to just launch to go from good to great!

Success Practice

Although I bashed the lean start-up method, I do agree with the idea of an MVP, or minimum viable product. An MVP is a product that has just enough features to gather validated learning about the product and its continued development. In other words, an MVP is your initial barebones product that you then change as you go.

I don't believe you even need an MVP to Just Launch. Instead, you just need the idea of an MVP. Whatever product or service you are thinking of creating, launch a website describing what it is and set a launch date three months from now. Setup a payment gateway for people to preorder your product or service. If you get people ordering your product or service, make sure you create your product or service. If you don't get anyone ordering your product or service, you don't have to build your product or service at all.

SUCCESS REVIEW

Which previous *Success Strategy* did you notice while I was discussing this one?

Do What You Know

Notice that I encouraged you to build a product or service that you yourself would buy. If you do this, you are essentially staying within the realms of what you know, and have immediately increased your chances of success.

Which other previous *Success Strategy* did you notice while I was discussing this one?

Use Parkinson's Law

Notice that I arbitrarily stated to set a launch date three months from now promising your product or service to customers. You might have thought, "Well, how can I be sure I can create the product or service in that time?" Parkinson's Law will assure that you do. When I launched the website for Prep Expert in February of 2011 promising a course in June of 2011, I did not have a course developed. But once I had eighteen students enroll in the pilot summer class, I definitely kicked into high gear to create a course. Just Launch and Parkinson's Law are intimately related.

Finally, this book is a manifestation of Just Launch. I wrote a blog post on January 31st, 2016 about the Law of Attraction and promised people that I would be releasing a book called *Self-Made Success* on April 30th, 2016 that had many more strategies. I started taking pre-orders for the book. But I didn't have a book. In fact, I didn't have anything written except that blog post. But I got preorders for the book. So you better believe that Parkinson's Law made sure that I wrote the book. In addition, I have not asked for one person's feedback about any of the strategies in this book. I'm simply launching the book. Just Launch and worry about iterations later.

ENTREPRENEURSHIP SUCCESS STRATEGY #5
NEVER GO TO A GUNFIGHT WITHOUT BULLETS

SUCCESS STRATEGY

Whenever you are entering a negotiation, you must have a backup offer. Whenever you are pitching an idea to investors, you must show some initial traction. Never show up to a gunfight without bullets in the chamber.

No matter what profession you are in, you will eventually have to negotiate. Always have one bullet in your chamber when you do: the backup offer. Negotiation is an art form. The best negotiators have spent years perfecting their craft. I won't try to explain every nuance of the art of negotiation here. But I will share the one strategy that has been most useful to me: the backup offer.

If you go to a negation without a backup offer, you are doomed. In a negotiation, there is you, Party A, and the other party in the negotiation, Party B. Both parties want to capture as much of the pie as possible. In order to capture more of the pie for yourself, threaten that there is a Party C who is willing to give you more of the pie than Party B is. But your threat has to be credible. If Party C is not as valuable, or worse—not even real—then this negotiation tactic will backfire.

On *Shark Tank*, one of the reasons I was unable to negotiate Mark Cuban down from the 20% equity that he asked for was that I didn't have a backup offer bullet in the chamber. All four of the other Sharks had gone out already. I actually think this is one of the reasons that Mark often waits to be the last Shark to make an offer. If all four of the Sharks go out on a deal, then the entrepreneur has no backup offer, or credible threat, to negotiate with. That's what happened to me.

When pitching an idea to investors (such as on *Shark Tank*), you need another bullet in the chamber: initial traction. Do not ever pitch an idea to investors without proving that it has worked. Even if you have only shown your idea to work on a small scale, that is better than not having any track record at all. One of the reasons I was successful on *Shark Tank* was that I was able to show that my classes worked on a small scale (in Las Vegas) and that there was huge potential to grow the company (both on the Internet and in larger cities such as Los Angeles, New York, and San Francisco).

Never go to a gunfight without at least two bullets in the chamber: a backup offer and initial traction.

SUCCESS EXAMPLE

When I want to rent out a conference room at an executive office suite in a new city to run SAT classes for Prep Expert, it is always a big negotiation. The executive office suite owner wants to charge me as much as possible for the conference room and I want to pay as little as possible. Here's an example of how having a backup offer bullet in my chamber helps me in these gunfights.

The first city we wanted to expand Prep Expert to after Las Vegas was San Diego. So we found a location in La Jolla that was very similar to the one we use in Las Vegas. When I contacted the owner about renting the location for our classes, he quoted me $50 per hour. For our 60-hour SAT prep course, that cost would be $3,000.

I didn't shoot my backup offer yet. It would be foolish to waste your bullet too early in battle. Instead, I explained the benefits he would gain by working with us. For example, I told him that we primarily use the conference room after business hours (after-school and on weekends) when the conference room is typically not going to be in use by his regular office clients. This would mean he's essentially creating revenue from an underutilized asset. In other words, free money. In addition, I showed some initial traction by telling him about the 20 to 30 courses a year in Las Vegas that we run and that this long-term partnership could result in hundreds of thousands of dollars in revenue for him down the line. After this initial negotiation, he reduced his price down to $25/hour or $1,500 per 60-hour SAT prep class—half of his original offer.

But I hadn't even pulled the trigger on my backup offer bullet yet. So I did some research. I found a similar conference room nearby to his location that would serve our purposes for $600 per class. I then made him an offer to run our classes at his location for $1000 per class or threatened that we would be going with the other location. In reality, the other location was not nearly as nice as his location. But of course, I didn't mention that.

The owner of our desired San Diego location agreed to my offer of $1000 per class—one-third of his original quote. All because I fired my most powerful bullet in the gunfight: a backup offer.

Success Practice

The next time you are in a negotiation, make sure you have a backup offer. But don't fire your backup offer bullet too early. First, get a sense of the playing field. Understand the other party's motivations and what they initially want. Next, explain the benefits of the agreement from the perspective of the other party. Then allow the other party to change their initial offer based on what you've said. Finally, fire your credible backup offer bullet. If you are not unreasonable, amazing things will typically happen.

The next time you are pitching an idea, make sure you have some initial traction. Obviously, showing sales is the best way to show initial traction. But if you don't have sales yet, there are other ways to show traction. Show number of website hits, a successful crowdfunding campaign, or some other kind of social validation for your idea. Don't be one of the many people in line with me at the open call audition for *Shark Tank* who just had an idea, but had not tried to implement it at all. They were dead before they even got to the gunfight; they just didn't know it yet.

Success Review

Which previous *Success Strategy* did you notice while I was discussing this one?

Capture the Whole Pie

This one was easy to identify because I explicitly mentioned splitting the pie. That's all negotiation really is: deciding how to divide a pie. By bringing bullets to the gunfight, you can capture more of the pie than you ever thought possible.

Which other previous *Success Strategy* did you notice while I was discussing this one?

Be a Big Fish in a Small Pond

This one was harder to spot. But when I described initial traction, it's really all about being a big fish in a small pond. If you can show that you can own a small pond (like I did with the SAT prep market in Las Vegas), then potential investors and partners will be more likely to believe that you can eventually own a big pond. Show initial traction by being a big fish in a small pond.

Entrepreneurship Success Strategy #6
Realize Bureaucracy Is the Root of All Evil

Success Strategy

A bureaucracy is an administrative system with many rules and policies. If you are an entrepreneur, you want to stay away from bureaucratic organizations as much as possible—they will try to stop you dead in your tracks.

One of the biggest benefits of being an entrepreneur is freedom. You are your own boss. You don't have to answer to anyone. You create the rules.

This is the polar opposite of being an employee in a large, bureaucratic organization. You have multiple levels of superiors. You have many policies you must follow.

Once in a while, entrepreneurs have to interact with bureaucratic organizations. You will find that any progress you attempt to make with a bureaucratic organization will typically be stifled by the policies and lack of creativity by the bureaucratic organization.

I have noticed this firsthand when I run Prep Expert and when I work in Los Angeles County Hospital as a third year medical student on rotations. At Prep Expert, I have the freedom to make things as efficient as possible. If a change needs to be made, I change it immediately. At LA County Hospital, it is virtually impossible to get anything changed because of the mountains of policies and paperwork.

Bureaucratic organizations are the root of all evil.

SUCCESS EXAMPLE

In 2012, I had been running Prep Expert for about a year. It was becoming successful in my hometown in Las Vegas while I was in medical school in Los Angeles. Because I was so busy in med school, I thought one of the best ways to scale the company would be to create a pre-recorded online SAT course taught by me. This way, students from around the world could learn from me at any time and I could still go through medical school as planned.

But there was one problem. McGraw-Hill now owned the copyright to my SAT content. So I couldn't publish an online SAT course without their permission. Instead of asking for it, I decided I would figure out that piece of the puzzle later.

I reached out to a dozen large test prep companies that I thought might be interested in partnering with me on such an endeavor. The owners of the world's largest privately owned GMAT preparation company, Veritas Prep, were interested. Chad Troutwine and Markus Moberg are two of the most dynamic and successful entrepreneurs I have ever met. With degrees from Harvard and Yale and a penchant for seizing big opportunities, they were on board right away.

After we had worked out the terms of our joint venture, there was only one step left: getting McGraw-Hill to bless off on letting us use the content from my book *SAT 2400 in Just 7 Steps* in the online course. Here's where we met the evil of bureaucracy.

McGraw-Hill is a $3 billion company with over 6,000 employees—the epitome of a bureaucracy. A lawyer who must have been the victim of bureaucracy himself gave me the following counsel:

> It won't be possible to use that material in an online SAT prep. ... McGraw Hill now owns the copyright to it ... and you are restricted from competing with McGraw Hill by creating other similar works ... you can't even lend your name to a competing product. At least you can't do any of these things without permission of MGH. Will they grant you permission? It's doubtful, no profit in it for them. MAYBE, if each online subscription came with a copy of the book they might bite, who knows though. It's a tough spot for you to be in, you basically have backed yourself into a corner and restricted what you are allowed to do in the SAT prep market.

That was very encouraging. But he was right. When we first approached the permissions and licensing departments at McGraw-Hill, they did not want to hear from us. (Note that if an organization has multiple departments, you are likely dealing with a bureaucracy.) They said they didn't do literary licensing agreements and would not be interested. When I asked my editor at McGraw-Hill for some advice on what to do, he said the following:

> Before going ahead with any such arrangement, we would need to study the legal, branding, and sales implications very closely. There are drawbacks as well as advantages to consider, and so far, McGraw-Hill has declined to associate its corporate brand with that of any third party. You can make a proposal to Scott Rogers if you wish, but before doing so, I'd advise you to run the specifics by me. That way, I can probably tell you if your idea is something that the corporation might actively consider.

Scott Rogers was the VP of Strategy & Business Development for McGraw-Hill Education. Given that he was near the top of the totem pole, I thought he might be a better person to talk to than the licensing and permissions department puppets that I was talking to. And with a response like the one I got from my editor above, there was no chance I was running my ideas by him first. I decided to reach out to Scott directly with the following proposal:

> Below is a partnership that will sell thousands of copies of my book SAT 2400 in Just 7 Steps (ISBN: 0071780998) every year to one company: Veritas Prep. This relationship will be mutually beneficial to both McGraw-Hill Professional and Veritas Prep.
>
> Veritas Prep is the largest privately owned GMAT preparation and admissions consulting provider in the world. Overall, it is only second to Kaplan and ahead of Princeton Review. Founders Chad Troutwine and Markus Moberg have been on the cover of Entrepreneur Magazine as well as featured in media outlets such as The Wall Street Journal, Bloomberg, U.S. News & World Report, and Businessweek.
>
> I approached Chad and Markus recently about doing an SAT prep online course together. I sent them links to my website (2400expert.com), my awards, and my book, SAT 2400 in Just 7 Steps, being published in July by McGraw-Hill.
>
> In the process of development, we came up with a great idea: offer SAT 2400 in Just 7 Steps as a companion manual to our online SAT prep course. This way, students would be able to reference the book during my video presentations. Every student taking the course would own a copy of the book.
>
> **McGraw-Hill Benefit**
>
> (1) <u>Wholesale Revenue</u> — The McGraw-Hill Companies will generate hundreds of thousands of dollars in sales that would otherwise be unrealized. Veritas Prep sells thousands of GMAT courses each year. It would be very beneficial to have Veritas Prep bulk purchase tens of thousands of copies of SAT 2400 in Just 7 Steps each year from The McGraw-Hill Companies.

(2) <u>Fusion Marketing</u> — Veritas Prep will spend hundreds of thousands of dollars marketing and branding the SAT prep course through online, print, and possibly TV ads. Essentially, SAT 2400 in Just 7 Steps would piggy-back on Veritas Prep's marketing prowess without McGraw-Hill's Public Relations & Marketing Department spending a dime.

(3) <u>Consumer Revenue</u> — Many students and parents who do not purchase the online course will purchase the book on their own through McGraw-Hill, Amazon, Barnes & Nobles, etc. Veritas Prep will also offer the book for separate purchase in its online store.

Veritas Prep Benefit

(1) <u>Content</u> — We would need permission from McGraw-Hill to reference and use material from SAT 2400 in Just 7 Steps in our online videos. This would make it easier for us than having to develop a different companion manual.

(2) <u>Distribution</u> — We would like to include the logo of Veritas Prep on the cover of SAT 2400 in Just 7 Steps (the cover has yet to be finalized) and a blurb about Veritas Prep inside the book. I will work with my editor on finalizing the cover of the book.

For a book from a first-time author that McGraw-Hill expected to sell less than 5,000 copies of in the first year, this presents a tremendous opportunity to exceed sales expectations and assure longevity.

I have spoken to McGraw-Hill Special Markets and understand that I receive no royalty from bulk purchases. I am willing to forfeit any personal financial gain because it will benefit book sales overall.

Our goal is to eventually build an online course that will compete with Kaplan and Princeton Review. And in doing so, we hope that *will open the door for McGraw-Hill to be a serious competitor to Kaplan, Princeton Review, and Barron's in the SAT prep book market. Princeton Review started with Cracking the SAT with distribution through Random House. We hope to start with In Just 7 Steps with distribution through McGraw- Hill.*

*Sincerely,
Shaan Patel
Author of SAT 2400 in Just 7 Steps*

*Chad Troutwine & Markus Moberg
Co-Founders of Veritas Prep*

The e-mail worked! Thankfully Scott Rogers had enough business sense despite the bureaucratic organization he was a part of to push the deal through. We sold thousands of Veritas Prep SAT Online Courses and tens of thousands of McGraw-Hill's *SAT 2400 in Just 7 Steps*.

Years later, I faced the wrath of McGraw-Hill's bureaucracy again when I was about to appear on ABC's *Shark Tank*. *Shark Tank* requested that McGraw-Hill sign an IP release so that ABC could display the *SAT 2400 In Just 7 Steps* book on TV during my pitch. I thought McGraw-Hill would be jumping at the opportunity to have the book displayed in front of 7 million Americans for free! But when I forwarded the release to the Senior Director of Contracts, Copyrights, and Permissions at McGraw-Hill's legal department, I got the following response:

This release isn't appropriate for what they need—it's basically giving them all rights to the book. I've attached our standard movie/tv show letter instead. Please send back to them and if it's acceptable, I can sign and send back to you.

I replied with the following:

I spoke to Shark Tank and all they need is rights to the cover art so that they can display it on TV. They are asking that the original intellectual property release form be signed still but that the top line say "SAT 2400 in Just 7 Steps Cover Art." That way, they only have rights for the cover art, not necessarily the entire book. Let me know if you would be able to sign the original form with this change.

My e-mail was met with the following response in big, bold, red letters:

Their release is just too broad; they would basically be able to use the book however they want, including saying it's a terrible book that no one should buy, and we have no recourse under this release.

Clearly, this McGraw-Hill legal department employee had never heard of, "All publicity is good publicity." So I did the only thing I knew how to do. I reached out to Scott Rogers again! Scott was very excited that the book could be on *Shark Tank* and tried very hard to get the legal department to see the light. But even he could not get McGraw-Hill to sign the IP release. You win some; you lose some.

Ultimately, we had to put these ugly cardboard covers on my book during my pitch on *Shark Tank* so that you couldn't see what book it was. The books were never shown on television. And McGraw-Hill lost out on hundreds of thousands of dollars in book sales. Bureaucracy is the root of all evil.

SUCCESS PRACTICE

To avoid bureaucracy as an entrepreneur, create a flat organization so that you don't have people reporting to managers. In addition, try to limit the number of policies. If you do have policies in place, don't be afraid to break them if it results in a greater good overall. One of the worst aspects of bureaucratic organizations is that outdated policies limit flexibility to change anything.

SUCCESS REVIEW

Which previous *Success Strategy* did you notice while I was discussing this one?

Use the Permission Principle

When I stopped asking my McGraw-Hill editor for permission is when things really went well for me with the McGraw-Hill and Veritas Prep deal. My editor told me to run the proposal I was going to send to Scott Rogers by him first. I didn't. Instead, I had enough of the bureaucratic hoops my editor was making me jump, so I sent Scott Rogers the proposal directly. I then asked my editor forgiveness with the following e-mail:

> *I kind of jumped the gun a little bit because I e-mailed Scott Rogers this past weekend (before I saw this e-mail to run it by you first). Sorry about that. But it seems like he is receptive to licensing the manual to Veritas Prep under the condition of a large yearly sales commitment by Veritas Prep as described in the proposal.*

It's always better to ask forgiveness than permission. However, notice that you have to be careful when using the Permission Principle with bureaucratic organizations. You don't want to break the law or do something wholly unethical. For example, when McGraw-Hill did not sign the IP release to show the book during my *Shark Tank* pitch, I didn't just go ahead and take the book on-air and show it anyway. That would've put me in a legal mess. Practice the Permission Principle judiciously.

CHAPTER 4
SOCIAL SUCCESS STRATEGIES

(1) It's Better to Be Interested Than Interesting
(2) Embrace Failure
(3) Be Fully Transparent
(4) Play to People's Self-Interests
(5) Kill with Kindness
(6) Don't Play the Comparison Game

Social Success Strategy #1
It's Better to Be Interested Than Interesting

Success Strategy

One of the keys to social success is to take a genuine interest in others. If you are curious about what others have to say, they will immediately take a liking to you.

I first learned about this idea from my AP U.S. History teacher. He would always say that his mother would tell him, "It's better to be interested than interesting." This stuck with me for a long time, but I never really practiced it.

I am an introvert and have never been good at socializing. I used to be very shy and would struggle to come up with conversation topics. If I did come up with a conversation starter, it would typically be about myself. This is not the key to socializing.

Instead, always put yourself in the other person's shoes. Think about what they care about. Think about what they are interested in. Think about what they are thinking. In other words, be genuinely interested in them.

This makes socializing so much easier. When you can find a topic that the other person really enjoys, your job is done. You likely won't even have to speak much after that because the other person will be so excited to share what they have to say.

This is essentially what Dale Carnegie's *How To Win Friends And Influence People* can be boiled down to. Find out what makes people tick and explore that. Not only will you become great at socializing with others, but you will also seem less self-aggrandizing by not always talking about yourself.

The best way to have great conversations is to talk about the other person's interests rather than your own. But don't get me wrong; being interested is only half the battle. You still need to be interesting. When appropriate, share relevant and interesting stories. Make it a two-way street. Don't go radio silent after a few questions.

Success Example

My favorite person in the world to have a conversation with is my good friend Chad Troutwine. Chad has the highest social and emotional intelligence out of anyone I have ever met (possibly IQ too). Part of the reason he is so dynamic is that he is completely genuine and always interested in the other person's endeavors.

Chad is a serial entrepreneur with degrees from Harvard and Yale. Has has a JD, an MBA, and a Master's in Public Policy. He scored a 790 out of 800 on the GMAT and got a perfect score on the ACT. He started Veritas Prep, the world's largest privately owned GMAT preparation company, while at the Yale School of Management, which has now done over $100 million in revenue. He is a movie producer who has made films such as the wildly popular documentary *Freakonomics*. In 2002, *Forbes* named him the Future Capitalist of the Year. He lives in a beautiful home in Malibu, drives around in a black Lamborghini (which he's since upgraded to a Tesla), and hangs out with billionaires such as Chris Sacca!

I consider him the most interesting man in the world (sorry, Dos Equis). Of course, Chad would never mention any of the above if you have the good fortune of meeting him. Instead, Chad will look you in the eye and make sure that you have his full attention and engagement in any conversation. If the most interesting man in the world can be so humble as to limit conversation about himself, shouldn't we all take a genuine interest in others when socializing?

SUCCESS PRACTICE

The next time you are at a cocktail party or networking event, here are five simple questions you can ask to get the conversation going:

(1) What do you do?
(2) What do you plan to do next?
(3) Where did you grow up?
(4) What do you like to do outside of work or school?
(5) What brought you to this event?

Once you find something that seems to really excite the person, keep talking about that. Once the person is hooked on a topic, you've done the hard part. Chances are, you won't say much during the rest of the conversation, but the other person will feel like you are a great person to talk to!

SUCCESS REVIEW

Which previous *Success Strategy* did you notice while I was discussing this one?

Use the Art of Storytelling

I mentioned that you still need to be able to tell relevant stories when being interested in others. If you require the people to talk too much about themselves, they may get exhausted. You can add value to the conversation by telling your own stories. But try to keep them about the topics that your audience (in this case, the other person) is interested in.

Social Success Strategy #2
Embrace Failure

Success Strategy

Your greatest strength is the failure you have endured. By embracing failure, you will have engaging stories to tell others.

People love the underdog story. Why do you think so many movies are about a person who seems to have no shot at succeeding, but against all odds makes it work anyway? People would rather hear about your failures than your successes.

See failure as an opportunity. Every time I fail at something, the disappointment is only temporary. I quickly remember that once I overcome this failure, I will have an inspiring story to share with others.

Embracing failure can make you very dangerous. It's impossible to shake you because you've transcended rejection. For example, if I do not match into a dermatology residency program next year when I apply (one of the most competitive specialties in medicine), I will not sulk in my sorrow. Most medical students would be crushed by such news. Instead, I will turn it into a great story to share with others later about how I was still able to succeed.

This strategy is great news for entrepreneurs because failure is so common. You will likely have multiple failed ideas and businesses before you find one that works. Even when you find one that works, you will likely get rejected multiple times by customers, suppliers, partners, etc. Little do you know that every failure you face now is just making for an even better story for you to tell later.

No one wants to hear a story about how everything came easy to you. Instead, people would like to hear about how you struggled to get where you are. Embrace failure to give them the best story about rejection they have ever heard.

Success Example

About a month after I went on *Shark Tank*, I contacted a reporter at *Business Insider* to do an update about the *Shark Tank* Effect and how Prep Expert was doing after the show. The reporter and I had some conversations at length about my upbringing, my aspirations, my business, etc. I made sure to talk to the reporter more about my failures than my successes.

One Saturday morning I woke up and my phone was exploding. People were texting me screenshots of their computer screens—the *Business Insider* article hit the front page of Yahoo!

The article title read:

> This perfect SAT scorer got rejected by the Ivy Leagues, but got on "*Shark Tank*" and is now backed by Mark Cuban

The article blew up. It got over a million hits. Our website traffic exploded and sales went through the roof.

The key phrase in the article title that served as click bait was, "Rejected by the Ivy Leagues." People were intrigued by someone who had failed first, then succeeded later. In addition, many people can relate to getting rejected by top universities and would love to root for someone who shares their struggle.

To share a little bit more color around these "rejections," I was rejected by Harvard and Princeton when I was in college. I did get into Brown, but the *Business Insider* reporter did not want to change the article title when I pointed that out. In addition, I was rejected by Harvard and Yale when I applied to medical school. I was rejected by Harvard and Wharton when I applied to business school. Stanford also rejected me for college, medical school, and business school. So it's been a recurring theme in my life! But hopefully I have convinced you that it's not the badge of the university that you wear that makes you. You can succeed regardless.

Moral of the story: embrace failure to tell the best stories.

Success Practice

List your biggest failures in your life. Then describe how you struggled through those rejections and why you felt like it was initially important. Next, describe how you were able to overcome these failures and succeed anyway. Now write this in a story format. You now have an inspiring story to share with others.

Success Review

Which previous *Success Strategy* did you notice while I was discussing this one?

Use the Art of Storytelling

Notice how I kept mentioning "stories." Failure stories are so much more interesting than success stories. People can relate to your failure because they too have failed. And if you have overcome that failure, then you can give them hope that they too can overcome their own failures.

Remember that a great story always starts with an "initial weakness." In this case, your failure is the "initial weakness." The Art of Storytelling and Embracing Failure go hand-in-hand. Make sure you have great failure stories lined up to inspire those around you.

Social Success Strategy #3
Be Fully Transparent

Success Strategy

If you are open and honest, people will be willing to be open and honest with you. Be fully transparent to genuinely connect with others.

People appreciate honesty more than ever. Social media allows people to paint an unreal life without any hardships or truths. Because transparency is so rare, if you offer it to others, it is like a breath of fresh air. And they will be willing to reciprocate that honesty.

This strategy is actually diametrically opposed to Law 30: Make Your Accomplishments Seem Effortless from Robert Greene's *48 Laws Of Power*. But Greene's book was written in 1998 before the advent of social media, smartphones, and a fully connected world. Today, it is almost impossible to hide. Privacy is almost non-existent. So it is best to simply be honest and transparent in the first place.

For example, there was a student at my high school who got a perfect score on the SAT the year before I did. He said that he never studied for the SAT and simply got a perfect score on the test. He was using the 30th Law of Power. By appearing to have accomplished one of the greatest standardized testing feats known to mankind without putting in effort, his aura of power increased. He seemed legendary. However, once word got out that he had studied quite extensively for the test, his power quickly faded. In fact, he looked silly for having lied in the first place.

When I got a perfect-score on the SAT, I let people know how hard I studied. I did the exact opposite of Law 30. But people appreciated the honesty and often enroll in my courses because they can relate to my SAT struggles. Be fully transparent in today's society—it's more important than ever.

Success Example

My best friend growing up, Anuj, was a great socializer. Everyone liked him. He was able to connect with just about anyone he met and they would tell him their deepest, darkest secrets.

I would be jealous that Anuj could get people to divulge such private information to him. As a middle-schooler, secrets and gossip were important. Of course, now I realize how silly it all was. But back then, I was just a kid without a clue.

I wondered how Anuj could get secrets from people whereas I couldn't. I now realize that Anuj practiced one of the principles of being fully transparent: Give A Secret To Get A Secret. Anuj would not only receive very personal information from others, but he would also first offer personal information about himself to others. I was the polar opposite. I was very private and very opaque. I hardly shared anything that was very personal. And this is why I failed at getting people to open up to me, but Anuj succeeded.

By initially giving a secret to others, it is almost an obligation for them to reciprocate. Of course, it doesn't always have to be a secret, necessarily. By simply being honest with others first, they have an obligation to be honest back. By being fully transparent, you have just opened up a highway to open and genuine conversations.

Success Practice

Think of something that you typically don't share with others. You may be embarrassed about it or believe that people will judge you for it. Now, share that thing with someone you trust. You will typically find that people respond very well to vulnerability. See how the other person responds. Did it open up a genuine conversation? Did the other person share something that makes him or her vulnerable?

Once you have shared this with one other person, try sharing with more. You should even consider writing a blog post about it. You will find that the more open and honest you are, the more positively others will respond to you. You will be a breath of fresh air in a world full of privacy, opaqueness, and insincerity.

Success Review

Which previous *Success Strategy* did you notice while I was discussing this one?

Embrace Failure

Being fully transparent requires that you sometimes have to be vulnerable. We are often vulnerable when we need to discuss our rejections and shortcomings. But as we learned previously, we should embrace failure. Do not shy away from the opportunity to be fully transparent about your biggest failures. You will encounter hundreds, thousands, or even millions of people who will appreciate your honesty.

Social Success Strategy #4
Play to People's Self-Interests

Success Strategy

Realize that everyone is self-interested. By appealing to others self-interests, you will get people to immediately take a liking to you.

No one cares about you as much as they care about themselves. While this is a cynical view of the world, it is true (barring perhaps parents, children, spouses, and siblings). You must use the self-interested aspect of human nature to your advantage.

This is why the golden rule is completely wrong. The golden rule states that you should "treat others as you would want to be treated." However, this appeals to your own interests, not other people's self-interests. For example, you may not care to receive flowers. But I'm sure your wife appreciates when you send her flowers because she likes them. That is why it is much more powerful to follow the platinum rule: "Treat others as **they** would want to be treated." In other words, appeal to people's self-interests.

I used to hardly ever think about other people's interests, only my own. I would always explain the benefits of something from my perspective. Similar to many teenagers, the world revolved around me. I could not have been more wrong with this world view.

As I grew older, I began to put myself in other people's shoes. I started to think about what they wanted and I began to have much better success in both social and business negotiations.

For example, I wanted to throw a *Shark Tank* viewing party at the high school I went to (my business is about SAT scores after all). In order to do so, I would have to ask Clark High School's principal. The old me would have gone into her office and talked about how *Shark Tank* was going to be a great opportunity for me. But the new, older me was wiser. I thought about what the principal wants: for her high school to be seen as the best in Las Vegas. So I played to her self-interests. I went into her office and explained how Clark High School would benefit from the local and national media surrounding *Shark Tank*. I saw her eyes immediately light up! She was immediately on-board with the idea but wanted to make sure the event was more about Clark High School than it was about me. I assured her it would be. I was able to host a 300-person viewing party for my *Shark Tank* debut for virtually free because I played to people's self-interests.

SUCCESS EXAMPLE

Airing on *Shark Tank* can be frustrating. After I taped the episode in June, the producers are very opaque about when your air date will be. They tell you that there is no guarantee that you will air on *Shark Tank* at all (only 70% of pitches actually air on television). If they choose to air your episode, they will call you two weeks before your episode is scheduled to air to inform you. Until then, you have to remain extremely tight-lipped about airing on the show. You cannot tell a single soul that you pitched on *Shark Tank*.

For a business that depends so much on scheduling, this can be very annoying. We wanted to open multiple new locations across the United States to coincide with the airing of my *Shark Tank* episode. I was pretty sure that the publicity from *Shark Tank* would help fill classes in many new markets. However, I didn't know when I would air. I was fairly certain we would air in the Fall of 2015, so a January 2016 start date made sense. To be safe, I set a start date of SAT classes in many new cities for January 15th, 2016.

However, we didn't air in the Fall. The way we set up our contracts with office locations is that we have the option to cancel our conference room booking rental two weeks ahead of time. So the two-week window for me to cancel without getting charged was dwindling down. I then got an e-mail from *Shark Tank* that we would be airing on January 29th, 2016.

In order to have enough weeks to prepare students before the March 5th New SAT exam and to capture the publicity of *Shark Tank*, I would have to start our classes on January 30th. But I wasn't sure if we would get enough students to enroll in our new cities to run a full class until after *Shark Tank* aired. So I had to get the office owners to agree to throw out the two-week cancellation clause because of the tough situation I was in.

But let's be honest—the office owners don't care about my situation, only their own. So I played to their self-interests. I sent them an e-mail explaining how I would mention their office location name in any local and national media publicity that I got from the *Shark Tank* airing. This certainly enthused many of them and they were happy to throw out the two-week cancellation clause.

SUCCESS PRACTICE

As described above, Play to People's Self-Interests whenever you are in a business negotiation. The other party only cares about how they can capture more of the pie, not how much of the pie you capture.

However, playing to people's self-interests can also be used in social situations. The next time you are trying to convince a friend to do something, think about what they really care about and capitalize on that.

For example, I've often had friends in medical school who refuse to go out on the weekend because they want to study the entire weekend. These friends care about studying. So I appeal to their self-interests by explaining how little actual studying they would get done on a Friday night, pointing out that breaks are essential to be refreshed for studying, and offering to spend the entire Saturday at the library with them studying. This usually results in my friends going out with us!

Success Review

Which previous *Success Strategy* did you notice while I was discussing this one?

It's Better to Be Interested Than Interesting

Playing to People's Self-Interests requires that you take an interest in their interests. Essentially, you must put yourself in the other person's shoes. You must become interested in a person to understand their motivations and aspirations. Being interested in others is the first step to playing to their self-interests.

Social Success Strategy #5
Kill with Kindness

Success Strategy

This is a defensive strategy. When another person commits a foul act against you, it is best not to reciprocate with a foul act in response. Instead, ignore the foul act, or even be kind, to such a misguided person.

As your success grows, you will have more people become envious of you, better known as "haters." These people will throw stones at you in the form of derogatory remarks and verbally abusive attacks in an attempt to unravel you. For an example of such people, simply scroll through the comments section of any celebrity's YouTube videos or Instagram photos and you are bound to find these Internet trolls. (It's much easier to unleash your vile remarks when you can hide behind an avatar and computer screen.) To neutralize such trolls, ignore them or respond with kindness. It's what they least expect.

Ghandi said, "An eye for an eye makes the whole world blind." Don't fight fire with fire. Put the fire out with water.

You can turn any negative disparagement into a positive one by simply agreeing with the other party, or even exaggerating it. This works particularly well for sarcastic comments that are not intended to be directly hurtful.

For example, in Indian culture there is an obsession with light skin. But I have dark skin. So I have definitely been made fun of for being so dark. It used to bother me tremendously. However, now I kill such comments with kindness by exaggerating them and turning them into a humorous joke. I respond with something like, "I'm Jay Z dark and just looking for my Beyoncé." Usually, the person who made the initial comment about my dark skin has nothing more to say. They expected me to get angry or become self-conscious with their belittling comment, but I didn't. Instead, I made their comment empowering—the exact opposite of their intention. Their plan backfired.

SUCCESS EXAMPLE

Near the end of 2015, I began to run into some trouble with one of my instructors at Prep Expert. He began to throw temper tantrums and was an unpleasant employee to manage. We put up a posting to hire another instructor. However, this instructor saw the posting and submitted a fake resume under a fake name to simply mess with us. (I think he had some larger mental health issues.)

How do I know the resume was fake? Because his real resume stated things like, "Winner of the Ivan Wood Memorial Scholarship in Economics, awarded to a student with a demonstrated ability in statistics and quantitative economic thinking." And the fake resume stated things like, "Awarded OSU's Ivan Wood Memorial Scholarship in Economics—monetary award for demonstrated ability in statistics, econometrics, and quantitative economic thinking." There were over a dozen similar instances of virtually identical lines between my troubled instructor's resume and the new instructor's fake resume. In addition, when we tried to schedule an interview with the "new" instructor, he'd always have to cancel the interview at the last minute citing an emergency. It wasn't exactly very hard to figure out that I was dealing with a troubled personality.

I could have fought fire with fire at this point. I could have confronted the instructor about submitting a fake resume and fired him on the spot. But given his erratic personality, I thought this would only lead to bigger issues. But I did decide that I would notify him that we would be letting him go on January 1st, at the start of the New Year, but that I wouldn't mention that I knew he submitted a fake resume to us.

On New Year's Eve, I got a voicemail from this instructor about how he was frustrated that he hadn't heard from me in a while. He also thought that I had blackballed him from the holiday party that we typically have at the end of the year since he didn't get an invite. Truth be told, we were too busy preparing for *Shark Tank* that we didn't have a holiday party this particular year. But his mind was making up stories, likely due to his mental health issues. I decided I would respond to the voicemail the next day and let him know that he'd no longer be working for the company—it was New Year's Eve after all and I was going out to celebrate.

About an hour later, I got frantic text messages and phone calls from my Director of Operations that her e-mail account had been hacked. Someone had gotten into her e-mail account and sent egregious e-mails to employees, parents, students, and office location owners. Here is an example of one of the e-mails sent to a parent:

Emma,

Please do not ever e-mail us again about your stupid faggot kid. They are a loser and will amount to nothing. You need to just face the facts and give up already. F*** off.

Prep Expert Director of Operations

I was sure it was this frustrated, and now clearly deranged, instructor who had left me a voicemail just a couple of hours before. He knew the generic password that I had set up for e-mail accounts, and unfortunately, my Director of Operations never changed hers.

At this point, I was furious! I was on my way to celebrate the New Year, and I could not have been angrier. I wanted to send this instructor many text messages about how I would be pressing charges, that I knew about his fake resume, and to expect a call from my lawyers.

But what would that have accomplished? He was clearly a mentally ill person. This instructor would fight fire with an even bigger fire. If I did press charges, he would likely escalate things even further—possibly physically harming me or one of my employees.

So I decided to kill with kindness. I wrote him the following e-mail:

Hi XXXX,

I got your voicemail expressing your concern about your future at Prep Expert. I had planned to respond yesterday, but we had to deal with an Internet hacking issue.

In any case, you are correct that your contract won't be renewed for the 2016 calendar year. It simply has to do with me pursuing a new strategy at Prep Expert.

Nevertheless, I really appreciate all of the work you have done for Prep Expert. You've certainly been a professional and autonomous tutor who never needed a lot of direction from me. I'm happy to write you a letter of recommendation for any job that you seek in the future. And I wish you the best of luck with your graduate school applications. I'm sure you'll be successful in whatever field you choose to pursue next.

Thanks,
Shaan

I was overly kind and played dumb as though I didn't know all about his indiscretions. He responded with the following:

Shaan,

Thank you for officially responding to my voicemail. I'm sorry to hear about the Internet hacking issue. I noticed that my password for my Prep Expert e-mail was also changed and someone had been in my account too. I changed my password as soon as I could to something stronger and, since I'm no longer working with you, I will probably delete my account altogether.

I do appreciate your guidance as well. You were a good mentor as well and really showed me how to teach, how to motivate a large crowd and, of course, how to take the SAT! I certainly couldn't have gotten this far without your help. I do wish you the best in that strategy you're pursuing, which I am sure will satisfy you greatly.

All the best,
XXXXXXX

I never heard from this instructor again. Sure, we had to do some damage control—increasing security on company passwords and apologizing to many people for the foul e-mails sent by a hacker. But we didn't lose much—no employees or customers left us. And I was able to put this huge fire out by killing it with kindness.

Success Practice

The next time you are attacked by someone, kill him or her with kindness. This is one of the hardest *Success Strategies* to practice because it requires you to use it when emotions are high. This means you must monitor your emotions and realize that your initial impulse may not be the correct response. When I got a phone call from my Director of Operations on New Year's Eve about the terrible e-mails that had been sent from her account, my initial impulse was to send my troubled instructor threatening text messages. But I had to monitor my emotions and pull myself back. I am glad I didn't send those text messages because it would have only escalated the situation further.

When someone says something to you that is abusive, do not respond by abusing the person back. Instead, do one of the following three things:

   (1) Ignore them
   (2) Respond with kindness
   (3) Exaggerate their misguided comment and add humor to it
       (best for sarcastic comments)

Kill with kindness to neutralize your opponents.

Success Review

Which previous *Success Strategy* did you notice while I was discussing this one?

The Power of Now

The Power of Now requires that you monitor your thoughts. You need to monitor your thoughts to Kill with Kindness. It's so easy to get angry and act on impulse when someone attacks you. Instead, use the Power of Now to monitor your angry emotions and Kill with Kindness.

Social Success Strategy #6
Don't Play the Comparison Game

Success Strategy

The comparison game is when you compare yourself to others. It is a losing game that always results in dissatisfaction. Avoid the comparison game at all costs.

The cause of unhappiness is not accepting your current state. If you can accept your current state, the unhappiness will vanish. However, if you play the comparison game, you will never accept your current state. In other words, you will never be happy.

In a social context, do not compare yourself to others. There will always be someone who has more money than you do, who is more attractive than you are, who is smarter than you are, etc. You cannot win playing the comparison game.

With respect to money, the comparison game is what leads to greed. Let's say you currently think making $100,000 per year is a lot of money. Once you make $100,000, you will meet people who are making $500,000 and you will compare yourself to them. Once you make $500,000, you will meet people who are making $1,000,000 and compare yourself to them. Once you make $1,000,000, you will meet people who are making $10,000,000 and compare yourself to them. And the comparison game goes on and on in a never-ending, vicious cycle.

The comparison game is ubiquitous in today's society because of social media. As we look at posts by our friends, we subconsciously compare ourselves to those posts. Are we as good looking as our friends? Are we having as much fun as our friends? Are we as happy as our friends? The answer to these questions is likely no because you are comparing yourself against an unreal snapshot of carefully-selected happy and exciting moments in other people's lives. This is likely why multiple studies have found that the more happy posts there are on social media, the crappier people feel about their own lives.

Stop playing the comparison game and you will stop the unhappiness. The first step to avoiding the comparison game is to accept yourself. It doesn't matter what imperfections you have. You have to accept your current state: physical appearance, monetary status, etc. If you don't love yourself first, you will prevent others from loving you. Be your own best friend. If you don't like yourself, no one will like you.

My 7th grade science teacher was once talking about Michael Jackson's multiple plastic surgeries, and said, "I don't care how you look, you need to eventually just accept how you look. You don't need to like it, but you need to accept it." She was talking about how becoming content with your current state will lead to greater happiness.

The next step to stop playing the comparison game is to accept others. You have to accept others for who they are, good or bad. This is similar to the saying, "To each his own." People usually don't have a hard time accepting people that are lesser than them in some way. For example, it's easy to accept someone who has less money than you because the vile emotions of jealousy and envy don't creep up. But it's harder to accept, love, and truly be happy for someone who has more than you in some way. For example, most people are jealous and envious of multi-millionaires and would rather see them fail than succeed further. Stop playing the comparison game, stop gossiping with toxic people in your life, and be happy for everyone (including yourself); whether they have less or more than you should be irrelevant. Because you have already accepted yourself, there is no need to want what others have.

Success Example

As I mentioned before, Indians are obsessed with light skin. Indian culture desires fair skin and despises dark skin. To me, it seems quite ridiculous that the amount of melanin in your skin determines how attractive you are considered to be. But this is due to the comparison game.

Images of beauty, especially in India, are always of fair-skinned individuals. Bollywood actors and actresses are all light-skinned. But the majority of the population in India is dark-skinned. This dichotomy causes the Indian population great anxiety. Because Indians play the comparison game against the images of beauty that are projected to them, India's skin-lightening cream market was estimated to be worth $432 million and growing at 18% per year in 2010.

As a dark-skinned Indian, I also used to play the comparison game, and it caused me great unhappiness. I wished I could be as light as some of my friends who were considered more handsome. The teasing from other Indians about my dark skin certainly didn't help. But I realize now that everyone was just playing the comparison game—and they were happy to be winning at it in this particular instance.

It wasn't until I began to accept my dark skin that I became much happier. I now don't mind my dark skin. And because I accept it, I find that others accept it. My relationships are more fulfilling because I don't play the comparison game.

SUCCESS PRACTICE

Choose something that you are unhappy about. To really practice this strategy well, choose something that you are unhappy about that you can't change. For example, you might be unhappy about your weight or finances, but those things can change. Height is a better example of something that people may be unhappy about that they can't change.

Now, accept whatever you are unhappy about. Find examples of other people who have succeeded despite having the same disadvantage that you currently perceive yourself as having. They will serve as great role models of how to not let your particular trait hold you back.

Practice accepting the things you don't like about yourself and stop playing the comparison game to increase your own happiness.

SUCCESS REVIEW

Which previous *Success Strategy* did you notice while I was discussing this one?

Embrace Failure

When you stop playing the comparison game, you need to accept your current state. When you accept your current state, you need to accept your current shortcomings, or failures. Although these failures may be no fault of your own, you need to accept them. In fact, you need to accept them so much that you stop perceiving them as failures or shortcomings. By avoiding the comparison game and embracing your shortcomings, you will reduce your own unhappiness, which will lead to having more fulfilling relationships with others.

CHAPTER 5
PRODUCTIVITY SUCCESS STRATEGIES

(1) Work Smarter and Harder
(2) Use Internal Motivation
(3) Start with a Morning Power Hour
(4) Listen to Audiobooks
(5) Turn Off the Tech
(6) Assign Accountability and Deadlines

PRODUCTIVITY SUCCESS STRATEGY #1
WORK SMARTER AND HARDER

SUCCESS STRATEGY

Work smarter and harder to accomplish more in a year than most people would in a lifetime. Become both the hardest working person in the room and the most efficient working person in the room.

One of my top instructors at Prep Expert's favorite sayings is, "Work smarter, not harder." I hate this saying (sorry Ryan)! I hate it because it implies that you can't do both. In other words, it encourages laziness. Instead, you should work smarter AND harder.

The most common question I get asked is, "How do you run a business and go to graduate school simultaneously?" There is no secret to how I work. I simply work harder and more efficiently than most other people. As my favorite Mark Cuban saying goes, "Work like there is someone working twenty-four hours a day to take it all away from you."

To work harder, stop making excuses. I don't believe in, "I don't have enough time." There is always enough time. You simply have to work harder and smarter with the time that you have. If you don't think there's enough time, then you need to make more time. I'll discuss how you can make more time in the *Success Example* and *Success Practice* that follow. Use the Navy Seal 40% Rule to stop making excuses. When Navy Seals think they're at a point of physical exhaustion, they tell themselves that they are really only

40% done. This gives them the mental energy needed to power through any task.

To work smarter, focus on your core competencies. Don't complete tasks that can be done by someone else or done by a software program for cheap. Don't complete tasks that you are not good at. Instead, complete the tasks where you add the most value.

Work smarter and harder to become more productive than you ever thought possible.

SUCCESS EXAMPLE

The summer before I started medical school, I had two major tasks to complete in two months:

> (1) Develop and teach the pilot class for Prep Expert
> (2) Finish writing *SAT 2400 In Just 7 Steps* for McGraw-Hill

Essentially, I had to launch a business and write a book in two months. As an added bonus, I also signed up to run the San Francisco Marathon the week before medical school started. So I had to train for that, too.

I felt completely overwhelmed. How was I going to get everything done before I started medical school?

On days that I was not teaching class, I would go to the library and write my book. I would stay from open until close and complete massive amounts of writing. I would then go run ten to fifteen miles at the UNLV track to prep for my marathon.

I was working hard, but it wasn't enough. I had to make time.

I realized that one of the biggest areas I spent time when writing was developing SAT questions for the book. However, this was also where I wasn't adding a lot of value. My value really came from developing the strategies students needed to approach the test. So I decided to focus on my core competency of writing strategies and hire out the test question writing.

I found freelancers on the Internet with previous experience writing test questions. I paid them to create the SAT questions for my book. I essentially created time by hiring someone else to do the task that was my biggest time waster.

But I didn't stop working hard. I continued writing SAT strategies every day, training for the marathon every day, and launching Prep Expert every day. I was working both hard and smart.

The result? I started medical school, trained instructors to teach future classes for Prep Expert, finished *SAT 2400 In Just 7 Steps*, and ran the San Francisco marathon all in the same week.

Work smarter AND harder!

SUCCESS PRACTICE

One tangible way to work smarter is to hire freelancers. Is there some menial task that you complete at work or school that could be done by someone else? Of course, don't hire out your core competency (although I have heard of a software programmer who hired a freelancer in China to do his entire job for him). To hire a freelancer, put up a job posting on UpWork.com. I recommend doing a fixed-price posting rather than an hourly posting since it's hard to monitor how many hours someone in the Philippines is working. The key to hiring a good freelancer is to ask for a sample of the work you are looking for first. You will get dozens (possibly hundreds) of applications for your posting, but only hire the freelancer that produces the best sample.

One tangible way to work harder is to only go out one night a week. If you are working on a Friday or Saturday night, then you are working when 99% of America is not. I'm not saying don't have a social life. I usually go out both Friday and Saturday nights. But when I have work to do or a deadline to meet, I limit my nights out to one night a week. This is one easy way to work harder than most.

SUCCESS REVIEW

Which previous *Success Strategy* did you notice while I was discussing this one?

Use the Pareto Principle

If you recall, the Pareto Principle states that 80% of all results is due to 20% of all effort. By working smarter (e.g., hiring a freelancer), you are spending less time on the 80% of effort that is typically wasteful anyway. By working harder (e.g., dedicating more hours to your core competency), you are spending more time on the 20% of effort that really matters with respect to building massive value. When you do both together, you can magnify the effects of the Pareto Principle to epic proportions.

Productivity Success Strategy #2
Use Internal Motivation

Success Strategy

In order to spend the number of hours necessary to become unbelievably productive, you will need to motivate yourself. It is impossible to work harder and smarter if you don't know what you're working harder and smarter for.

Set clear and tangible goals. For example, "I want to lose weight" is not a clear and tangible goal. However, "I want to lose ten pounds" is a clear and tangible goal. Stop being so abstract with your goals. Be as specific as possible.

There is a difference between internal motivation and external motivation. If someone else wants you to do something, they may provide external motivation. But this is far less effective than internal motivation. Internal motivation is when you yourself want to do something because you have a particular goal you want to accomplish. Internal motivation is necessary for massive productivity.

We often encounter the clash between internal and external motivation at my company Prep Expert. When parents want their student to do well on the SAT, but the student himself is not motivated to do well on the SAT, then it usually doesn't end well. The external motivation of the parent is not aligned with the internal motivation of the student.

This is why I encourage students to motivate themselves by creating a desire to do well on the SAT. In order to do this, they need to have a clear and tangible goal they want to achieve with a high SAT score. No one wants a high SAT score just to have a high SAT score. There should be something the student is trying to achieve with that high SAT score. Will a high SAT score help her get into a particular college? Will a high SAT score help her get a particular scholarship? Or will it help her become eligible for athletics at a particular university? All of these are good reasons for why a student may want a high SAT score. By always keeping the ultimate goal in mind, students are able to motivate themselves to put in that extra hour of SAT prep necessary to do well on the exam.

Success Example

When I was in high school, I always kept my ultimate goal in mind. After volunteering at a local hospital emergency department in high school, I was inspired to become a physician. The traditional way to get into medical school in the United States is to go to college as a premed student, maintain a high GPA (often above 3.7), get a high MCAT score, do basic science research, volunteer overseas, and often take one to two years off between college and medical school to continue doing research. Then you apply to medical school and might get in—it's extremely competitive with acceptance rates that are often less than 5%. This is a lot of work and uncertainty!

Therefore, I thought it would be great if I didn't have to worry about getting into medical school if I could just get acceptance into a BS/MD program. BS/MD programs offer high school students a guaranteed spot in med school. This meant no stress about applying to med school in college. Many of these programs don't require you to take the MCAT, the GPA requirements are manageable (often around 3.0), and some even reduce the total number of required years of college and medical school. There are approximately 50 programs around the country at different universities. Some of the well-known programs are at Northwestern, Brown, and Boston University.

The one that I went to at USC was unfortunately discontinued. But these programs are essentially a great deal for students who want to become physicians. (By the way, these combined programs also exist for law, pharmacy, dental, and other professional graduate degrees.) However, the acceptance rate at BS/MD programs is often less than 5% and the minimum SAT score was often 2200 (approximately 1500 on the New SAT). It was this goal that helped me stay motivated throughout the SAT preparation process. If I did not know exactly why I wanted a high SAT score, I surely would not have been able to raise my SAT score 640 points from a 1760 to a perfect 2400.

In addition, don't just dream of your goal—visualize it. There is a difference between a dream and a goal. A dream is something you don't think is possible. A goal is something you believe is possible within a certain timeframe. When you look at your goals, they should motivate you.

Keeping your tangible goals in mind is what will keep you productive when it seems like all of your friends are out having so much fun. Now, more than ever, it's easy to get FOMO (fear of missing out) because of social media. But all of your hard work and preparation will eventually be worth it. All you need to do is motivate yourself, work hard, and visualize your goals.

SUCCESS PRACTICE

To motivate yourself, start with the WHAT, then focus on the HOW.

WHAT do you want to accomplish? Write it down as though you have already accomplished it. Visualize how your life would be if you accomplished it. Try to imagine how it would feel to accomplish this task. Make sure this is something that you want to accomplish, not something someone else wants you to accomplish. Remember, internal motivation is ten times more powerful than external motivation.

HOW are you going to accomplish it? Once you have determined what you want, begin your research. Learn about all of the steps necessary to accomplish your goal. If you are really internally motivated to accomplish this goal, you will be willing to take the steps necessary to get there.

Even if it is a long, arduous process to get what you want, you will always have something to keep you going: internal motivation.

Success Review

Which previous *Success Strategy* did you notice while I was discussing this one?

The Law of Attraction

This was an easy one to spot. Motivating yourself to accomplish your goals requires use of the Law of Attraction. We discussed the concepts of writing goals down, believing they have already been accomplished, visualizing goals, and feeling the effect of your goals in the very first part of this book about the Law of Attraction. Use internal motivation to never give up on your goals so that you become unbelievably productive.

Productivity Success Strategy #3
Start with a Morning Power Hour

Success Strategy

The ultimate secret to productivity is to do one hour of work right after you wake up. If you don't have an hour to spare in the morning, wake up one hour earlier than you usually do. Voila! Now you have time for a morning power hour.

The morning power hour is a powerful tool to increase your productivity, if you use it wisely. To get the most out of your morning power hour, do the one task that you hate doing the most or the one task that is most difficult to do. For example, replying to e-mails is probably not a good task to do in your morning power hour. Replying to e-mail is not very mentally taxing and should be saved for later in the day when your mind's energy is winding down.

When you complete the most arduous task first, your whole day changes. Suddenly, you feel accomplished at 6:00, 7:00, or 8:00 a.m.—a feeling that few people have that early. This sense of accomplishment will carry over to the rest of your day. You will be ready to tackle even more when you get to the office or to school. The confidence that the morning power hour produces is almost as valuable as the output of work that it produces.

This is why you should also try to avoid starting your day with a meeting. For the most part, meetings are a waste of time. Most meetings should be e-mails. By starting your day with a meeting rather than doing another power hour when you get into the office, you are draining your productivity. For example, I have a quick stand-up meeting in our office at 10:00 a.m., not 9:00 a.m. This allows me to do my morning power hour before I get into the office. Then I do another power hour from 9:00 a.m. to 10:00 a.m. By the time we have a quick meeting at our office, I have completed a tremendous amount of work through two morning power hours.

I don't believe people who say, "I work better at night" or "I'm not a morning person." No one is a morning person. Everyone would like to sleep longer if they had the opportunity. But if you force yourself to do work in the morning, you will find something amazing happens. You will accomplish twice as much in one hour as you would in two hours during the normal workday.

This happens for a few reasons. First, your mind is freshest in the morning. It has just been revitalized by a good night's sleep. Second, it is one of the most quiet times of the day. There is usually very little noise in the morning and you can really concentrate on the task at hand. Third, there are usually few distractions from social media or text messages. Avoid checking your phone until after your morning power hour. You will find that you haven't missed anything because most of the world is not awake yet.

SUCCESS EXAMPLE

Ask any medical student what the worst part of medical school is and the answer will always be the same: studying for Step 1 of the United States Medical Licensing Exam (USMLE). This is an eight-hour test that covers virtually every detail related to anatomy, behavioral sciences, biochemistry, microbiology, pathology, pharmacology, physiology, and interdisciplinary topics such as nutrition, genetics, and aging. To add to the pressure, your Step 1 score determines what specialties you can apply for in residency. If you don't get a high Step 1 score, you can kiss your dreams of dermatology, ophthalmology, and plastic surgery goodbye. Students often spend over a thousand hours studying for Step 1.

I split up my Step 1 studying into two main tasks: reading and practicing. Reading new material related to the USMLE was the hard part because it required complete attention and focus in order to try to remember every detail of what I read. Practicing USMLE questions was much easier because it was just applying what I was reading to practice problems.

Therefore, I decided to do a morning power hour that consisted of reading new USMLE material when I was studying for the exam. I estimated that I could read approximately twenty pages in one hour. So every morning, I would wake up early and immediately flip open a USMLE study guide and start reading. I found that I absorbed the material much better in the morning than any other time of the day. After my morning power hour, I would go to the library and continue my reading power hours. But I felt so much better and accomplished about my day because I started it off with a morning power hour.

SUCCESS PRACTICE

You may be thinking that you can't practice this strategy because you don't have an extra hour of time in the morning. So I'm going to help you create one. I too hate waking up early. But if I need to be ultra-productive, morning power hours are essential.

Here's how to create a morning power hour: set your alarm for one hour earlier than usual. For example, if you typically wake up at 7:00 a.m., set your alarm for 6:00 a.m. Go to bed half an hour earlier than usual so that you only lose half an hour of sleep. If you think it's too much work to wake up earlier, consider this: if you spend 8 hours a day sleeping, you spend one-third of your life asleep (approximately 27 years); but if you spend 6 hours a day sleeping, you spend one-fourth of your life asleep (approximately 20 years). You've essentially added 7 years to your life by sleeping just a little bit less.

Now, how can you prevent yourself from hitting the snooze button too many times? Place your phone on the other side of the room. By putting your phone across the room, it requires you to physically get out of bed. You won't hit snooze if you are standing up and walking around just to get to your phone. Quickly brush your teeth and wash your face.

Now, get to work. Complete the task that is typically most mentally taxing or the one that you usually try to avoid doing. Notice how much easier it is to do during your morning power hour compared to any other time of day.

I believe a morning power hour is twice as productive as a working hour during the normal business day. If you do a morning power hour every business day, you have just added ten hours of productivity to your workweek. Congratulations!

Success Review

Which previous *Success Strategy* did you notice while I was discussing this one?

Work Smarter and Harder

The morning power hour is a manifestation of working smarter and harder. The morning power hour requires you to work harder because you are getting less sleep and adding work time to your day. It requires you to work smarter because you are getting work done when your mind is in its most efficient state.

This book is also a manifestation of the morning power hour. As I stated earlier, I wrote this entire book over the course of my two-week spring break during business school at Yale. I typically wake up at 7:30 a.m. However, I knew that I needed to be extra efficient during this particular spring break. So I implemented what I always do whenever I have to be massively productive: the morning power hour. I set my alarm for 6:30 a.m. every day over spring break. Doesn't sound much like a spring break, does it? During my morning power hour, I write one entire *Success Strategy* (the Strategy, Example, Practice, and Review). Over the course of two weeks, I wrote fourteen *Success Strategies* strictly during morning power hours. That means that almost 1/3 of this book (14 out of the 48 *Success Strategies*) was written in fourteen hours—that's the power of the morning power hour!

Productivity Success Strategy #4
Listen to Audiobooks

Success Strategy

To rapidly increase your knowledge, productivity, and wealth, listen to audiobooks during your daily commute. No matter how busy you are, you should be able to read at least one book per week—approximately 50 books per year.

Given how many books I have referenced throughout *Self-Made Success*, you might think that I am a bookworm. But nothing could be further from the truth. I used to hate reading. As a teenager, I would even be so naive as to brag about how I didn't read anything outside of what was assigned for school. (This is probably why I initially struggled with the SAT Reading section so much.) Even for books that were assigned for school, I often didn't read them (SparkNotes was my best friend). Yes, teenager Shaan was an idiot. Now I realize that reading books outside of school is not only interesting and fun, but that it is also essential to becoming a better person.

I have always been a slow reader. This is part of the reason that I disliked reading so much. Combine the fact that teachers often assigned books that I was not interested in with the fact that I was a slow reader to begin with, and it makes sense as to why I was not a fan of books.

In addition, I also have very little extra free time to read for leisure. But this is everyone's excuse for why they don't read more. So I figured out the way to read a massive number of books without spending any extra time out of my day reading: audiobooks.

I used to listen to music in the car, on the train, on my walk to school, on a plane, etc. Now, I listen to audiobooks. Audiobooks have expanded my mind across every discipline. I cannot believe how much more progress I have made in the last two years towards becoming a happier, healthier, and wealthier person than I did during the first twenty-four years of my life. My only regret is not taking up leisure reading earlier in life.

Reading blogs or listening to a podcast can certainly be helpful, but is in no way more insightful than full-length books. Authors spend much more time and effort creating books than they do writing blogs or taping podcasts. And the quality of content that you find in books reflects that.

What is the best investment you can make? Books. The best investment you can make is not real estate, stocks, bonds, gold, etc. Instead, the best investment you can possibly make is in yourself. With every other investment, you rely on someone else to create value so that you can capture a small sliver of the pie. But when you invest in yourself, you are responsible for creating the value pie so that you can capture all of it. And books are by far the best way to invest in yourself. I cannot tell you how many books sparked ideas that I implemented in my business Prep Expert that have led to hundreds of thousands of dollars in additional revenue—now that's an ROI (Return On Investment).

The most successful people in the world are voracious readers. Mark Cuban reads three hours every day. Bill Gates reads a book every week. Warren Buffet spends 80% of his day reading. It's no coincidence that the most incredibly successful people on this planet read all the time. You have to consume new information constantly to stay ahead of the curve.

Now I understand that you likely go to work or school full-time and don't have a lot of time for reading. But that's the beauty of listening to audiobooks during your commute—you can get the benefit of reading books without spending any extra time doing so.

SUCCESS EXAMPLE

I primarily listen to nonfiction books and think you should too. Although fiction books are generally more popular for leisure reading, they don't spark the same number of life hacking ideas as nonfiction books. Sure, fiction books have life takeaways. But these implicit lessons are few and far between compared to the explicit takeaways of nonfiction books.

I primarily listen to self-help and business books. Self-help books help me grow as a person mentally, emotionally, and spiritually. Business books help me grow my business to increase revenue, customer and employee satisfaction, and scalability. Combined, I have been able to see tangible gains in all aspects of my life.

Of course, I do occasionally read other books as well. Here is a complete list of the audiobooks that I have listened to this past year (I would recommend all of them):

(1) *The Road Less Travelled* by M. Scott Peck
(2) *The 4-Hour Workweek* by Timothy Ferris
(3) *The Life-Changing Magic of Tidying Up* by Marie Kondo
(4) *Tribes* by Seth Godin
(5) *The Four Agreements* by Don Miguel Ruiz
(6) *Platform* by Michael Hyatt
(7) *The Road to Character* by David Brooks
(8) *Never Eat Alone* by Keith Ferrazzi and Tahi Raz
(9) *Ask* by Ryan Levesque
(10) *MONEY Master the Game* by Tony Robbins
(11) *The Law of Success* by Napoleon Hill

(12) *How To Win At The Sport Of Business* by Mark Cuban
(13) *The Body Fat Solution* by Tom Venuto
(14) *Rework* by Jason Fried and David Heinemeier Hansson
(15) *Coupon Crazy* by Mary Potter Kenyon
(16) *The 48 Laws Of Power* by Robert Greene
(17) *Choose Yourself!* by James Altucher
(18) *Free Marketing* by Jim Cockrum
(19) *The New Rules of Marketing & PR* by David Meerman Scott
(20) *Think And Grow Rich* by Napoleon Hill
(21) *The Power Of Your Subconscious Mind* by Joseph Murphy
(22) *SEO 2016* by R.L. Adams
(23) *The Confidence Gap* by Steven Hayes
(24) *The Innovator's Dilemma* by Clayton Christensen
(25) *Google AdWords for Beginners* by Corey Rabazinski
(26) *Mark Cuban: The Maverick Billionaire* by Sean Huff
(27) *E-mail Marketing That Doesn't Suck* by Michael Clarke
(28) The Bhagavad Gita by Ekanth Easwaran
(29) *Delivering Happiness* by Tony Hsieh
(30) *Beyond Bigger Leaner Stronger* by Michael Matthews
(31) *The Gifts of Imperfection* by Brené Brown
(32) *The Power of Now* by Eckhart Tolle
(33) *Duct Tape Marketing* by John Jantsch
(34) *Creating Customer Evangelists* by Ben McConnell
(35) *The Secret* by Rhonda Byrne
(36) *The Secrets of the Millionaire Mind* by T. Harv Eker
(37) *Inbound Marketing* by Brian Halligan
(38) *The Worry Cure* by Robert Leahy
(39) *Modern Romance* by Aziz Ansari
(40) *Growth Hacker Marketing* by Ryan Holiday
(41) *Epic Content Marketing* by Joe Pulizzi
(42) *Scrum* by JJ Sutherland
(43) *How To Win Friends And Influence People* by Dale Carnegie
(44) *How To Stop Worrying And Start Living* by Dale Carnegie
(45) *The 80/20 Principle* by Richard Koch
(46) *Zero To One* by Peter Thiel
(47) *Purple Cow* by Seth Godin

(48) *The Hard Thing About Hard Things* by Ben Horowitz
(49) *Hooked* by Nir Eyal
(50) *Book Launch* by Chandler Bolt
(51) *Outliers* by Malcolm Gladwell
(52) *David And Goliath* by Malcolm Gladwell

SUCCESS PRACTICE

To practically implement listening to audiobooks into your life, start by figuring out what you're interested in. Go on Amazon and search topics that interest you. For example, I may search terms such as "Internet marketing," "spiritual growth," or "entrepreneurship." Look for books in the bestseller lists since these will likely be good reads. In addition, books on bestseller lists are typically offered in audiobook format.

Once you have identified an audiobook you would like to listen to, purchase it from Amazon. You will need an Audible account in order to listen to the book, so create one. If you are first-time Audible user, Amazon will usually give you the first audiobook for free!

Now download the Audible app onto your smartphone. Once you log in to your Audible account in the app, you should see the book that you purchased. The last step is to change the speed at which the book is played. I typically can understand a book if it is played at 1.5x speed. This will help increase your efficiency. The other great thing about the Audible app is that it keeps your place when you click pause on an audiobook. It was always annoying trying to find my spot again on audiobooks that I used to listen to in MP3 format on iTunes. That problem is gone with the Audible app!

The average American commute is one hour. The average audiobook length is six hours. If you listen to audiobooks at 1.5x speed, you can finish a book every four days. Of course, if you don't have a 30-minute commute to and from school/work (for a total of one hour of listening a day), you will need to find some other time in the day to do some listening. Start today!

Success Review

Which previous *Success Strategy* did you notice while I was discussing this one?

Work Smarter and Harder

Listening to audiobooks is just one example of the work smarter and harder philosophy. Listening to audiobooks requires you to work harder because you are reading more books than 99% of the population. Listening to audiobooks also requires you to work smarter because you are not losing any time out of your day by simply listening to audiobooks during your commute.

Productivity Success Strategy #5
Turn Off the Tech

Success Strategy

When you are looking to produce massive value, turn off the tech. This means your laptop, phone, or other electronic device should either be out of sight and out of mind or disconnected from the Internet.

I am addicted to my phone. In Nir Eyal's book *Hooked*, he explains how many of the social media apps that we all use have actually become habits that are hard-wired into our brains. I actually don't even realize how often I'm checking my e-mail, text messages, and Facebook. And I'm guessing neither do you. And since habits like these are hard to break, it's better just to avoid them altogether by turning off the tech.

In the world of Facebook, Instagram, Twitter, and Snapchat, distractions are all around us. You should disconnect from the Internet, phone, and any other technology that may distract you. Because information is so readily available to us at all times of the day, it's hard for many of us to find time to concentrate without interruption.

Turning off the tech is useful when you need to produce massive value. In terms of work, you may need to write a proposal, read a white paper, or do some other task that requires complete focus. Work that is not that mentally taxing may not require you to turn off the tech.

For example, replying to e-mail is not a work task that I consider mentally tasking. Not only can you not reply to e-mail without the Internet, but it's also a mundane task that doesn't require a lot of concentration. This is why I always reply to my e-mails at the end of the day when my mind is most mentally taxed. I also reply to e-mail in batches, every day or two. Sending e-mails every five minutes is a waste of time. Not only can most people wait a day or two for a response, but it also wastes your time to constantly check e-mail and reply to it because it's distracting you from producing real value at work. Hence, another reason why you should turn off the tech when working.

Another instance when you need to be massively productive is when studying. After having gone through high school when I prepared hundreds of hours for the SAT, having gone through college as a premed student, and having gone through most of medical school, I've learned a thing or two about studying. I've learned that the most effective studying occurs when I turn off distracting technology. This means turning everything off or at least putting it away—out of sight, out of mind.

When studying, all you really need is paper and a pencil. Hundreds of years ago, this is how people accomplished monumental tasks—whether it was writing books or studying for exams. It's probably no coincidence that people were much better writers and studiers back then. So if they studied hundreds of years ago without technology, you can certainly study today without all of the distracting technology. While I think technology has done great things for education, I also think it has become the biggest distraction to effective studying.

Technology is really a blessing and a curse. It's amazing to have so much information at your fingertips at any given moment, but it's also dangerous to have our minds get distracted by all of that information all the time. It's our responsibility to use technology wisely and not let it become counterproductive to accomplishing our work. So turn off the tech when you want to be ultra-productive!

SUCCESS EXAMPLE

The perfect place to accomplish a massive amount of work where the tech is already turned off for you is on an airplane. Whenever I travel on an airplane, I never purchase Internet. Not only is it very expensive, but it would also just serve as a distraction. Instead, I download all of the documents that I need to accomplish my work before I get on the airplane.

I am always surprised by how many people waste time on an airplane—sleeping, watching TV, etc. The airplane is my productivity powerhouse. I have accomplished monumental tasks in this Internet-less haven. For example, when I was preparing to film for *Shark Tank*, my producer asked me to put together 25 potential questions that I thought the Sharks would ask about my company and my responses to those 25 questions should they be asked. So on a flight from New York to Las Vegas (approximately five hours), I wrote the entire document and sent it to my producer for review. My producer said it was the best set of questions he had ever received from a *Shark Tank* entrepreneur and that he would be using my Q&A document as an example for future *Shark Tank* entrepreneurs. I don't attribute it to my writing skills. I attribute it to being in a no-tech, distraction-free zone when I was creating the document.

Similarly, the entire outline for this book was completed on a flight from New York to Las Vegas. On one five-hour flight, I outlined all 48 strategies and examples that I would be writing about in *Self-Made Success*. Creating a detailed outline of what I planned to write about made writing this book so much easier. Once again, I used my time on an airplane where the tech is turned off to produce massive value.

Success Practice

Obviously, you can't always be on an airplane when you want to get real work done. But there are a couple of things that you can do to mimic an airplane environment so that you are disconnected from the Internet.

First, physically separate from your phone. I get so distracted by Facebook, Instagram, Twitter, Snapchat, text messages, and e-mail notifications. Even if you turn off notifications on your phone, it's likely that you will be tempted to pick it up to start checking the latest updates if it is within arm's reach. This is why it's best to put your phone somewhere that you can't reach it immediately. For example, during my morning power hour, I will leave my phone on the other side of the room. During a normal workday, I will put my phone in my bag. You can also try putting your phone in airplane mode too, but it's so easy to take airplane mode off if your phone is sitting right next to you.

Second, turn off the Wi-Fi on your laptop or computer. I understand that most work is done on a computer nowadays. So I'm not saying you have to start doing your work with paper and pencil. Instead, disconnect from the Internet. And don't reconnect until you have completed one solid hour of work. You will be amazed by how much you are able to accomplish when you are not bombarded by e-mails, text messages, Facebook notifications, etc.

While physical separation from your phone and turning off the Internet may sound extreme, you will be surprised at how much more effective you are when you turn off the tech.

Success Review

Which previous *Success Strategy* did you notice while I was discussing this one?

Start with a Morning Power Hour

I briefly mentioned the morning power hour above. I also mentioned how completing work in one-hour chunks of time with no Internet can produce massive value. The morning power hour is so much more effective when you turn off the tech. You may be tempted in the morning to start browsing the news, Facebook, e-mails, stocks, etc. Instead, physically separate from your phone and turn off the Internet to maximize the value potential of your morning power hour.

This book is also a manifestation of this strategy. As I write every chapter of this book, my Internet is turned off and my phone is not within arm's reach. Turning off the tech can produce massive value, such as this book!

Productivity Success Strategy #6
Assign Accountability and Deadlines

Success Strategy

To increase your productivity and that of your team, assign accountability and deadlines. Make sure that each person knows exactly which tasks they are responsible for completing and by what deadline.

All of the previous *Productivity Success Strategies* have been related to solo productivity. But more often than not, you are not completing a task by yourself. Instead, you have to work in a team—whether it's a work team or a study group—to accomplish a task.

Managing a group of people is much more difficult than managing yourself. This is part of the reason that I went to business school. I have always been really bad at project management and working in teams. This is primarily due to me not ever having had a "real" job. I've always been in school and never worked for anyone else. So I don't have first-hand experience working in a large corporation. And frankly, I'm not sure that I want to. But after attending business school and managing full- and part-time staff for the past five years, I have learned two key principles to increase productivity in a team: assign accountability and assign deadlines.

Assigning accountability means that a particular task is a particular person's responsibility. Do not spread the responsibility of a task across multiple team members. If multiple people are responsible for doing something, no one is responsible for doing anything. If a task is too large for one person to complete, break the task into smaller parts. Then assign each smaller task to individual people within the team.

Assigning deadlines means that there is a particular date by which the person needs to complete his or her assigned task. Try to make the date challenging to hit, but still reasonable. It's best if you and the other team member mutually agree upon the date of completion for a particular task. In addition, a "definition of done" should also be specified. Discuss what the final deliverable should look like. If you don't discuss your "definition of done," then the person completing the task might turn in something that is very different from what you expected.

There are hundreds, if not thousands, of other important concepts and principles related to project management. But the two that I have found most important have been assigning accountability and assigning deadlines.

Success Example

I went to business school for a very unique reason. I have no plans of becoming an investment banker, management consultant, or working for a large corporation. Instead, I had one main motive when I decided to go to business school: to learn how to expand my business—Prep Expert.

Because I have no formal business background, I thought that a graduate business school education would serve me well. After three years, I was able to take Prep Expert from an idea in my head to the largest test preparation provider in Las Vegas. However, I had bigger aspirations. I wanted Prep Expert to be one of the largest test preparation providers in the world.

Was going to business school the right decision? I believe the answer is yes. While most detractors would argue that entrepreneurs do not need to go to business school, I would assert that the formal knowledge I have gained in accounting, economics, marketing, operations, and finance have helped me run a more efficient organization.

However, the most valuable class I took in business school was not part of the core curriculum. I took a class called Management of Software Development taught by Professor Kyle Jensen—the Yale School of Management's Director of Entrepreneurship. I originally took the class simply because of my fascination with mobile apps. Little did I know how transformative this class would be to Prep Expert.

Professor Jensen taught us about the principles of lean, agile, and scrum methodologies. These project management techniques are commonly applied in Silicon Valley tech companies to complete software projects. However, the ideas of rapid iteration, scrum sprints, and user experience were foreign to me. Common to all of these project management architectures were two key principles: accountability and deadlines. For example, scrum assigned accountability by assigning "user stories" (work tasks) to specific team members and assigned weekly or bi-monthly deadlines to those tasks (depending on how long each "sprint cycle" is).

Management of Software Development changed how we run our business at Prep Expert. We now use the agile architecture for project management in the office. Creating user stories and recording scrum velocities for non-software based projects has resulted in our office becoming more productive than ever.

Of course, many will argue that I didn't need to go to business school to learn about lean, agile, and scrum methodologies. But I can guarantee that I would not have taken these management techniques seriously if I had not been immersed in them for eight weeks.

Since implementing scrum, we have had record-breaking revenue every month since inception. In less than a year, the increased revenue generated will likely pay back the cost of business school. So can business school be a good investment for entrepreneurs? Yes.

Success Practice

Assigning accountability and deadlines does not have to be limited to a team environment. If you are a solo entrepreneur, you can still apply these principles to significantly improve your own productivity.

First, assign accountability to yourself. Create a prioritized list of tasks that you need to complete. Make sure that you are responsible for completing these tasks and that you don't spread the accountability of the task by sharing it with someone else.

Second, create your own deadline for each task. This is especially important for an entrepreneur. In school, your teacher will create deadlines for you. At a job, your boss will create deadlines for you. But if you work for yourself, no one will create deadlines for you. So it can be easy to let things drag on and on unless you set deadlines for yourself. Try to challenge yourself as much as possible with your deadlines and really stick to them.

Success Review

Which previous *Success Strategy* did you notice while I was discussing this one?

Use Parkinson's Law

Recall that Parkinson's Law states that "work expands to fill the time available for its completion" or that "work contracts to fit in the time we give it." I mentioned above that you should try to set challenging deadlines, both for yourself and for team members. This is essentially using Parkinson's Law. By assigning challenging deadlines to you and your team members, everyone will get more accomplished in less time than they ever thought possible.

CHAPTER 6
MENTAL SUCCESS STRATEGIES

(1) Practice Self-Control
(2) Track Progress
(3) Realize You Are Not This Body ... or Mind
(4) Have Faith
(5) Treat Entitlement as the Enemy
(6) Conquer Insomnia and the Fear of Death

Mental Success Strategy #1
Practice Self-Control

Success Strategy

The most universal and accurate predictor of success is not IQ, emotional intelligence, or vision. Instead, it is self-control. If you want to be successful, you need to manage emotions, delay gratification, and work hard. All of which requires significant self-control.

Do not let emotions control you. Far too often, I see people act impulsively on emotion. Instead, monitor your emotions. This is easy to theorize about, but much harder to practice when you are actually angry, upset, or experiencing some other powerful emotion. But try your best to practice enough self-control to be even-minded, to re-evaluate the situation rationally, especially when emotions are high.

You only have a limited amount of self-control. I often notice that when I have a big exam to study for or a big project to complete for work, I have a hard time eating a healthy diet too. It is really hard for me to choose a salad over a pizza when I am stressed. But when I have an open schedule, it is much easier for me to eat healthy and go to the gym. This is due to our self-control. Pick and choose your battles carefully—what items do you want most? Practice enough self-control to get them.

Possessing self-control is harder than ever today. Technology has added numerous distractions to our daily lives: e-mail, text messaging, Facebook, Instagram, Snapchat, Twitter, YouTube, Netflix, etc. Having the self-control to avoid all of these enticing platforms is no easy task. If you want to experience massive success, practice enough self-control to turn off the Internet, silence your phone, and work in a distraction-free environment.

Dr. Victoria Brescoll at the Yale School of Management inspired this strategy. She gave a guest lecture on personal change during an MBA leadership course. Professor Brescoll pointed to a famous Stanford marshmallow experiment as proof that self-control is crucial to success.

In the 1972 experiment, researchers placed a four- to six-year-old child in a room with just a marshmallow. The children were told that they could eat the one marshmallow now, but if they waited fifteen minutes, they would be rewarded with two marshmallows. This experiment was conducted on over 600 children. Only a third of the children were able to exercise enough self-control to delay gratification and not eat the marshmallow immediately. Years later, these children were found to be more successful based on a variety of life outcomes:

- Scoring 210 points higher on average on the SAT
- Earning higher salaries
- Being more popular with peers and teachers
- Having lower BMIs and better overall health
- Possessing fewer drug and alcohol problems

Many other studies have corroborated the findings of this study that self-control is a massive predictor of achievement. What's the secret to success? Practice self-control.

Success Example

I hated my body type growing up. As a child, I was chubby, even fat. After I hit puberty, my growth spurt got rid of the chubbiness. However, I didn't lose all of the fat. Instead, I had a body type that many Indian men have—the dreaded "skinny-fat" body.

Skinny-fat refers to your arms and legs being skinny but your abdomen being fat. With a loose t-shirt on, I didn't look that bad. But without a t-shirt, I had a donut around my waistline—all of the fat was concentrated around my abdomen.

I believe being "skinny-fat" is worse than being skinny or fat. If you are just skinny, then you can benefit from weight-lifting and eating more because you will pack on muscle and can afford to gain fat. If you are just fat, then you can benefit from exercising and dieting because you will have muscle to show after you have lost the fat. But changing a skinny-fat body type is much more difficult.

Transforming the skinny-fat body type is a two-step process. First, you need to lose the fat around your abdomen. Second, you need to slowly put on muscle being careful not to add too much fat back around your abdomen.

By the end of my junior year in college, my skinny-fat body was at its worst after years of eating fast food and not going to the gym regularly. So I decided I was going to change it.

First, I would have to lose the fat around my abdomen. To do this, I practiced an incredible amount of self-control with both my diet and exercise routine. I stopped eating fast food, began cooking, and limited my portions. I exercised every day straight for 180 days. Even when we took a family vacation to Europe, I would wake up at 4:30 a.m. to go on an hour run or hit the hotel gym. I ran my first long-distance run: the Malibu half-marathon. Although I had lost my abdominal fat and could see my abs for the first time in my life, I was also ultra-skinny.

So the second step would be to add muscle. I began eating more, supplementing my diet with whey protein, and weight lifting using progressive overload. I finally began to put on muscle that I never had before. Although I never got to be "buff," my body type completely transformed. All because I practiced enough self-control to regulate what went into my mouth as well as the intensity of my physical activity.

It was much easier to practice self-control my senior year of college than any other time in my young adult life because I was not taking difficult classes. Instead of applying my self-control to study as I always had, I applied it to my body. And the results were astounding—I was no longer skinny-fat!

I still reap the benefits of that year of ultra-healthiness today. I am more conscience about my diet and physical exercise. I have never lost all self-control that my body reverted back to being skinny-fat. I also picked up healthy diet and exercise habits that allow me to maintain, build, and cut when I need to.

Success Practice

Here's one simple mental tactic you can use to practice enough self-control when dieting: eat until you are satisfied, not until you are full. If you are like me, then you might have a tendency to overeat. To prevent this from happening, consciously think about whether you are satisfied with the amount of food you have eaten. Don't eat until your stomach is bulging!

One tangible way to do this is simply not to eat everything that is on your plate. If you have a sandwich, don't eat the last bit. If you are eating pizza, don't eat the crust. If you have a dessert, only eat half of it. This practice is especially difficult for me because my mom always raised me not to waste food. While I understand where she is coming from, I also don't believe that the little bit of food that I leave on my plate will help feed a hungry person. It will either go in my stomach and contribute to fat storage, or it will go in the trash. I choose the latter.

SUCCESS REVIEW

Which previous *Success Strategy* did you notice while I was discussing this one?

Turn Off the Tech

This one was easy because I explicitly mentioned that you should practice enough self-control to turn off the Internet and other technological distractions in order to be ultra-productive. But there was another *Success Strategy* that was more implicit ... did you notice it?

Use Internal Motivation

In order to *Practice Self-Control*, you must *Use Internal Motivation*. You must know the ultimate goal. If you haven't identified the clear and tangible goal that you are working towards, it will be difficult to delay gratification enough to get there. *Use Internal Motivation* to keep you on track in your effort to *Practice Self-Control*.

MENTAL SUCCESS STRATEGY #2
TRACK PROGRESS

SUCCESS STRATEGY

To accomplish any task effectively, you must track progress. Without tracking progress, you will be less likely to possess the mental endurance necessary to accomplish your goal.

Ignorance is bliss. If you do not keep track of your progress towards a goal, that goal becomes a dream. For example, let's say that you have a goal to run a marathon. If you do not track your progress by logging how much farther you have run from one practice run to the next, then you may never increase your distance from five to eighteen miles (note: you typically don't run a full twenty-six miles until race day when training for a marathon). Your goal of running a marathon just became a dream.

You must track progress in order to be extraordinarily successful at anything you do. Tracking progress can be used to accomplish monumental achievements across multiple disciplines.

With respect to academics, you should track the progress of your studying. Whenever I sit down for a few hours of studying, I track exactly how much I should be accomplishing each hour. For example, I may set a goal of completing 200 practice questions in a week for a particular subject. I then track my progress by making sure I complete 40 practice questions in one hour each week. Doing so not only assures that I accomplish my goal, but it also provides a mental confidence boost on day three when I have completed 120 questions because I know that I am making regular progress towards my ultimate goal.

With respect to reading, you should track the progress of listening to audiobooks. For example, I set a goal to listen to one audiobook each week. Let's say that the audiobook I plan to listen to is 7.5 hours long. This means I must listen to an hour and a half of the audiobook each day for five days. Given that I listen to audiobooks at 1.5x speed, I need to spend one hour of time listening to this audiobook. Given that I spend 20 minutes driving to work, 20 minutes driving to the gym, and 20 minutes driving back home, all I need to do is listen to the audiobook while I'm in the car. Each day, I track my progress to make sure that I have completed 1.5 hours of the book so that I can complete the book by the end of the week. If I did not track my progress, I start listening to Drake in the car, which would prevent me from completing my goal of an audiobook a week!

With respect to project management, tracking progress is also necessary. Scrum, an agile project management technique traditionally used to develop software products, has the principle of tracking progress baked directly into the workflow. Tasks are measured using a point system called "story points." The more "story points" that a particular task has, the larger the task is. At the end of each work cycle (called a "sprint"), the number of story points a team completed is examined (called "velocity"). The goal is to increase your "velocity" each week so that you are more efficient and productive with your time. However, the efficiencies of scrum would not be possible if tracking progress was not built into the system using story points.

SUCCESS EXAMPLE

Tracking progress is perhaps most powerful in the discipline of fitness. Changes in your physical appearance do not happen overnight. Therefore, tracking progress is essential to accomplishing any major fitness goal.

When I lost 30 pounds over the course of six months in college, I tracked everything. I tracked how much I weighed every morning. I tracked how many calories I was eating with every meal. I even tracked how much my food weighed using a scale to measure how many grams were in each serving. (Okay, this was a little extreme.)

But whenever I have wanted to accomplish a fitness goal (whether it was losing fat or gaining muscle), I have only been successful when I tracked my progress regularly. I get a mental confidence boost knowing that I only ate 1600 calories in a day rather than guessing that I didn't eat very much that day.

I have failed to accomplish my fitness goals when I don't keep track of my progress regularly. Remember, ignorance is bliss. If I plan to lose weight, but don't regularly weigh myself—I never lose weight. My goal of losing weight becomes a dream because I don't get the mental confidence boost of seeing regular progress towards what I want.

Success Practice

By far the best way you can apply this strategy is to buy a bathroom scale and weigh yourself daily. Doing so will immediately help you accomplish any fitness goal that you have.

If you would like to lose ten pounds, but you see that your weight is half a pound more one morning, this can seriously affect you mentally—in a good way! You will be more conscious of what you eat that day and perhaps will even exercise more.

SUCCESS REVIEW

Which previous *Success Strategy* did you notice while I was discussing this one?

Listen to Audiobooks

This one was easy. I explicitly mentioned that you can *Track Progress* to improve your ability to effectively complete listening to more audiobooks. However, there was another *Success Strategy* that was implicitly discussed. Did you notice it?

Assign Accountability and Deadlines

When you track progress, you are essentially becoming accountable to yourself. When I require that I listen to an hour and a half of an audiobook in a day, I am holding myself accountable to the progress that I would like to track. In addition, I am assigning myself a daily deadline for the progress I would like to track. Use *Assign Accountability and Deadlines* and *Track Progress* to accomplish more than you ever thought possible.

Mental Success Strategy #3
Realize You Are Not This Body ... or Mind

Success Strategy

There are three parts to you: a body, a mind, and a soul. Avoid becoming too attached to your body or mind. Try to identify with your soul instead.

In Sunday school growing up as a child, I would often attend lectures of the most profound religious text in Hinduism, the Bhagavad Gita. One of the big takeaways from the Bhagavad Gita is that we are not the bodies that we inhabit on this earth. Too often, people become attached to their physical body. But the Bhagavad Gita asserts that it really does not matter what your physical body looks like because your true self is a spirit soul that only occupies this body for a temporary amount of time. I always thought that this was a particularly useful insight.

It wasn't until much later in life that I came across an even more powerful insight: I am also not this mind. De-identifying from the body is a relatively easy concept to grasp. But de-identifying from the mind is a much harder concept to understand. Everyone believes that they are the mind.

But imagine that you have a higher self that goes above and beyond your mind: the soul. The soul is a separate entity from your mind and body. Think about the implications of this. Your true self is not all of the thoughts that occupy your mind all day long.

This mental strategy can help you tremendously. By detaching from your mind, you now shouldn't trust everything that you think. Try to become a third-party, objective observer of the thoughts that occur in your mind. By doing so, you will become more rational and even-minded.

SUCCESS EXAMPLE

Airing on *Shark Tank* is a stressful process because you never know if you will air. Even after you tape the episode, the producers don't tell you whether they think your segment will air on television. Instead, they just tell you that they will call you two weeks before your air date if your segment is selected to air. Only 70% of the segments that they tape actually air. This means there's an almost 1 in 3 chance that you can go through the entire *Shark Tank* process and never air at all. In addition, you cannot tell anyone that you went on *Shark Tank* if you don't air. You wouldn't get the benefit from the *Shark Tank* Effect—getting the attention of 7 million Americans for fifteen minutes on a Friday night during primetime television. The monetary value of such exposure is estimated to be equivalent to $9 million in marketing spend.

So after I taped my *Shark Tank* episode in June of 2015, I began to patiently wait. Every day, I would anxiously hope for a phone call or e-mail from the *Shark Tank* producers that my segment was going to air on television in two weeks. As you can imagine, I was biting my nails, because if I aired, it would completely change my business and life!

This is when my mind began to play tricks to me. I thought I might not air for a number of reasons. Maybe the producers didn't like my segment? Maybe the producers found some copyright issue? Maybe the producers taped way too many good segments? The list of reasons for why I might not air went on-and-on. As each week went by that I didn't get a phone call or e-mail, I started to get extreme anxiety that I was not going to air.

How did I get rid of this anxiety? I began to separate myself from my mind. I realized that I should stop identifying with the thoughts that were going through my mind. Instead, I tried to objectively observe my thoughts. My soul decided that my mind was likely playing tricks on me, which was causing me unwarranted anxiety. Once I de-identified from my mind, I became much more at ease. I no longer worried about the anxiety-provoking thoughts that were going on in my mind. I just calmly waited and detached from the result.

I got an e-mail on January 11th, 2016 that I would be airing on *Shark Tank* on January 29th.

Success Practice

I am not an expert at meditation, but one of the reasons that people enjoy meditation so much is that it provides an outlet to connect with their soul and detach from their mind.

One exercise you should try when meditating is to monitor your thoughts. Try to become an objective observer of the thoughts that are going on in your mind. Imagine that your thoughts are floating by on a river and that you are simply observing them as they go by on this stream. Do not jump in the river and get entangled with those thoughts. In other words, try not to let the thoughts affect you.

This is an exercise that you should not limit to meditation. As you go about your daily activities, try not to become too attached to the thoughts that go on in your mind. Remember that the mind that so many people identify with is really not your true self. You will become more even-minded and less likely to become a victim of your mind's emotions.

SUCCESS REVIEW

Which previous *Success Strategy* did you notice while I was discussing this one?

Use the Power of Now

I originally realized that I was not this mind after reading Eckhart Tolle's *The Power of Now*. While the main takeaway of the book was to focus on the present moment, an equally important concept is to de-identify from your mind. *The Power of Now* requires that you monitor your thoughts. But realizing that you are not your thoughts is just as important!

MENTAL SUCCESS STRATEGY #4
HAVE FAITH

SUCCESS STRATEGY

Have faith in a purpose larger than yourself. Having purpose will bring meaning to your life and allow you to have richer experiences.

Having faith doesn't necessary mean that you need to have faith in God. That is up to you. I will say that I too once doubted the existence of God. But the more I learned in medical school, the more I believed in a higher power. In my opinion, human physiology is just too perfect to have not had a designer. From hormonal feedback regulation to blood clotting mechanisms to electrolyte balance through ATPases, it all works perfectly without any programming. British scientist Lord William Kevin once said, "If you study science deep enough and long enough, it will force you to believe in God." This is certainly true for me.

Even if you are an atheist, you still need to have faith. In fact, you may need to have more faith than a believer in God. You need to have faith in randomness. You need to believe that human physiology, gravity, emotion, and the Earth being the perfect distance from the Sun are all random. Now that certainly takes faith!

Not having faith in purpose can have detrimental effects on your life. You may believe that you are a victim. When you are a victim, you become helpless and stressed. You think that no one can help you and that all bad things happen to you for no reason at all.

Instead, have faith. Have faith that everything happens for a reason. This will allow you to mentally cope with any rejection much more effectively. For example, I really wanted to attend Harvard Business School. But I was rejected. While I was disappointed, I had faith that everything will work out for the best. And I was right! Because I attended Yale, I was only an hour and a half from New York City for the *Shark Tank* open call audition that eventually led to a partnership with Mark Cuban. If I had been at Harvard in Boston, I may not have attended that open call audition in New York and pitched to the same casting call producer that moved me to the next round of auditions. So if I had to choose between attending Harvard or establishing a lifelong business partnership with Mark Cuban, which would I pick? Definitely the latter. Have faith that everything happens for a reason.

Success Example

When I was seven years old, I almost died.

My parents, my brother, and I went on a family vacation to Florida. We were visiting my dad's aunt who lived there. She suggested we go to the beach. This was my first time at the beach as a child, so I was very excited.

My dad's aunt, her daughter, and I went into the water while my parents and brother stayed on the shore. We were holding hands and having a lot of fun letting the waves hit us. Slowly we began going further out into the water until the water was waist-level.

Suddenly, the floor beneath us vanished and the current of the tide pulled us out further into the ocean. None of us could swim. We began panicking and yelling for hope. I remember holding onto my aunt, but we were sinking fast.

As the waves kept crashing on top of us, I remember crying and saying, "We're going to die." My dad's aunt kept yelling "Hare Krishna" (God's name in Hinduism). I began swallowing large amounts of salt water because I could not get my head above the water.

The next thing you know I felt something lift me out of the water and I could breathe air again. A nearby surfer had grabbed me and put me onto his surfboard. He took me back to shore and I lay on the beach for some time while I vomited all of the salt water out. The surfer and his friend also brought my dad's aunt and her daughter safely back to shore. I was in complete shock after the incident and couldn't speak for hours.

I owe my life to those surfers. My dad said there were no lifeguards on duty—he tried to find some as he could see us drowning. But my parents and brother also did not know how to swim. So they couldn't swim into the ocean to help us. My dad said the surfers who saved us came out of "nowhere."

If those surfers hadn't been in the area, I would have died. Once the lungs are full of water instead of air, oxygen deprivation kills the brain within three to four minutes. I have no choice but to believe that everything happens for a reason after being as lucky as I was to survive an experience such as this one.

Success Practice

The next time you experience disappointment, rejection, or things simply not working out, shrug it off. Accept that things will not always go the way you planned them. Have faith that everything happens for a reason and that your temporary unhappiness will actually be the best thing in the end. By associating purpose with every action, your life will take on a tremendous amount of meaning.

This is also why there is no reason to worry about future outcomes. Again, you can't control what will happen in the future. But you can control how you react to it. Ask yourself, "What's the worst that could happen." Then, try to take steps to prevent that from happening. But even if the worst-case scenario does happen, accept it, and remember that everything happens for a reason. The worst case will likely be the best case in the long run—you just can't connect the dots as to why yet.

Success Review

Which previous *Success Strategy* did you notice while I was discussing this one?

Embrace Failure

When you have faith that everything happens for a reason, then it's very hard for failure to disturb you. If you begin to view failures as having purpose, then you don't become as irked by them as others would. Having the faith to embrace failure and believing that everything will work out makes you mentally unshakeable.

Mental Success Strategy #5
Treat Entitlement as the Enemy

Success Strategy

Entitlement is the enemy of success. No one owes you anything. The minute you believe you are entitled to a handout, you have lost the game.

Treat every project that you work on like it is the first one you have ever worked on. People tend to work harder on the first project than any other because they are hungry for success. If you are successful with the first project, you may not work as hard on the second project because you have already tasted success.

Complacency is the peril of success at an early age. For young people who have experienced some level of success, never lose that hunger that came with the very first project you ever worked on. If you become complacent with your accomplishments, you become vulnerable to entitlement. This is likely one reason that so many child actors struggle to succeed as adult actors. They become too comfortable with the success they had at such a young age that they don't put in the work necessary to succeed as an adult.

Never call yourself the CEO. I can't stand when a founder of a new startup calls him- or herself the CEO of a company. By calling yourself the CEO, you are immediately giving yourself an undeserved entitlement that will likely set you up for failure. Be humble enough to curb your ego and roll up your sleeves to build a company that one day you will be proud to call yourself the CEO of. But for now, be the founder, not the CEO.

I am usually never too sure of myself. Some people have very strong convictions and are sure that their positions are correct. These people would probably not be great startup founders. As an entrepreneur, you should always have some level of paranoia that you could lose it all tomorrow. There's confidence and there's overconfidence. Don't be so entitled that you have too much of the latter.

You should not only Treat Entitlement as the Enemy with respect to work, but you should also treat experiences as the enemy. The world does not owe you anything, either. Try to appreciate the great weather outside like it is the first time you have experienced sunshine; or a scoop of ice cream like it is the first time you have had such a decadent, sugary dessert. You are not entitled to these experiences.

If you treat every experience like the first time you have ever experienced it, you will be much more grateful for it and ultimately much happier. This is actually what children do. A child may be fascinated with the most mundane of objects because he has never seen it before. He is grateful for experiences because he does not feel entitled to them. Be grateful for even the most ordinary experiences because you are not entitled to them.

The recipe for success and happiness is to get rid of entitlement, be humble, and practice gratitude.

Success Example

My favorite music artist of all-time is Jay Z. I enjoy his music because it's about his rags to riches story: going from a drug dealer in Brooklyn to a media mogul worth $650 million. His business endeavors have included a clothing line (Rocawear), a part-ownership in an NBA team (Brooklyn Nets), and a record label (Roc Nation). His music about hustling to get to the top is likely why Jay Z is a favorite among many entrepreneurs.

But what is perhaps most intriguing about Jay Z is the longevity of his music career. He released his first album, *Reasonable Doubt*, in 1996. Since then, he has consistently put out quality music for the past twenty years. Few artists can last for more than a few years, especially in today's ultra-competitive Internet music world. How has Jay Z been able to remain relevant for so long? By Treating Entitlement as the Enemy.

The closing record from Jay Z's *Black Album* is called "My 1st Song." He starts the song with an audio clip from Notorious B.I.G. saying that, "The key to staying on top of things is treat everything like it's your first project." The entire song is about Jay Z's approach to music: treating every song like it is his first song. In other words, Jay Z has been able to endure for so many years while thousands of other artists have faltered because he Treats Entitlement as the Enemy despite his massive success.

Success Practice

Here's how you can Treat Entitlement as the Enemy, no matter who you are.

- As a student, treat every assignment like it is your first assignment.
- As an employee, treat every workday like it is your first day on the job.
- As a serial entrepreneur, treat every business like it is the first business you have ever started.

- As an author, treat every book like it is the first book you have ever written.
- As a musician, treat every song like it is the first song you have ever composed.
- As a blogger, treat every blog post like it is the first blog post you have ever blogged.
- As a coder, treat every project like it is the first project you have ever developed.
- As a designer, treat every design like it is the first design you have ever created.
- As a human, treat every experience like it is the first experience you have ever had.

Success Review

Which *Success Strategy* did you notice while I was discussing this one? Actually, it would be impossible for you to notice. But this book is actually a manifestation of the Treating Entitlement as the Enemy.

I have written almost 10 books at this point in my career, but my first book will always be very special to me. Because I had to prove myself to a publisher who had initially rejected my book proposal, I wanted to make sure I wrote the best SAT prep book the world had ever seen. As a first-time author, I was hungry for success. I approached every day with the following question in mind: "How can I write something today that will be more amazing than any other SAT prep material students have ever seen?"

Despite having sold nearly 50,000 books now and having a few my books hit #1 in various Amazon categories, I have never let entitlement get the better of me. I continue to have the same hunger to write incredibly impressive books for readers every time I sit down to write a new one. For this book, I was not complacent with my past successes and continued to approach every day with the following question in mind: "How can I write something today that will be more amazing than any other self-help material readers have ever seen?"

I never lost the initial mindset that brought me success with books in the first place. So if you think *Self-Made Success* is good, it's because I Treat Entitlement as the Enemy.

Mental Success Strategy #6
Conquer Insomnia and the Fear of Death

They say sleep is the cousin of death. So I've combined how to conquer insomnia and how to conquer the fear of death into one strategy. You will find that they are more similar than you think.

Success Strategy: Conquer Insomnia

To conquer insomnia, stop thinking about the next day. Many people cannot fall asleep at night because their mind is full of thoughts about tomorrow. Stop worrying about the future and you will get much more restful sleep.

According to WebMD, one in four people suffer from insomnia, which is equivalent to 80 million Americans. In the United States, insomnia is responsible for 252 million lost days of productivity and $63 billion in annual financial losses to the economy.

Without a good night's sleep, it would be difficult to practice many of the *Success Strategies* in this book. For example, it would be hard to Start with a Morning Power Hour at 6:00 a.m. if you couldn't fall asleep until 3:00 a.m.

To fix this problem, the best solution is not medication. Instead, you need a mental hack. The one that I have found most effective is to stop thinking about tomorrow's worries. Instead, focus on what is in front of you right now—a comfortable bed and pillow and nothing to do but relax. It's quite the luxury. If you take tomorrow's responsibilities with you to bed, you will have a hard time sleeping. Instead, do not let anything come to your mind—try to erase all thoughts, past and future, from your head. Just focus on the present moment.

SUCCESS EXAMPLE: CONQUER INSOMNIA

I used to struggle with insomnia. In college, I would often find that I couldn't fall asleep until 3:00 or 4:00 a.m. I would then have the worst day. Not only would I be extremely tired, but my body would physically ache, my mind was sluggish, and all I could think about was how horrible I felt.

I tried multiple different solutions. First, I tried taking NyQuil (essentially, diphenhydramine). This helped sometimes, but not always. I then discovered melatonin. I thought this was great because it was natural! Melatonin is the hormone your body naturally secretes to help you fall asleep. I used melatonin for years, and it generally worked well. But I became addicted to melatonin. I felt like I couldn't fall asleep without taking it. I also got worried that my body would stop naturally secreting melatonin if I kept taking exogenous melatonin because I might shut down the negative feedback loop. Eventually, melatonin started to fail me too.

I had to get to the root of my insomnia. That's when I read Dale Carnegie's *How To Stop Worrying And Start Living*. Carnegie asserts that thinking about yesterday or tomorrow is the root cause of worry. Instead, people should focus on today.

I applied this philosophy to my bedtime routine. I stopped letting my mind run wild with thoughts about both yesterday and tomorrow. As I fell asleep, I used to be worried about the exam that I would have the next day, the project I needed to complete the next day, or the hundred things I needed to accomplish the next day.

But after reading Carnegie's book, I stopped worrying about the next day when falling asleep. All I cared about was the present day. And suddenly, my insomnia vanished. I no longer need to take melatonin to fall sleep. I can now fall asleep within minutes (instead of hours). I couldn't be more grateful for this mental hack of focusing on the present moment that has helped me conquer insomnia.

SUCCESS PRACTICE: CONQUER INSOMNIA

Here's the exact technique you can use to focus on the present moment in order to conquer insomnia. I adapted this routine from *The Power Of Your Subconscious Mind* by Joseph Murphy.

When you lay in bed at night, start by relaxing each body part from toe to head:

- Focus on your *feet*, then completely relax them, and enjoy this comforting feeling.
- Focus on your *ankles*, then completely relax them, and enjoy this comforting feeling.
- Focus on your *legs*, then completely relax them, and enjoy this comforting feeling.
- Focus on your *knees*, then completely relax them, and enjoy this comforting feeling.
- Focus on your *thighs*, then completely relax them, and enjoy this comforting feeling.
- Focus on your *hips*, then completely relax them, and enjoy this comforting feeling.
- Focus on your *abdomen*, then completely relax it, and enjoy this comforting feeling.

- Focus on your *lower back*, then completely relax it, and enjoy this comforting feeling.
- Focus on your *chest*, then completely relax it, and enjoy this comforting feeling.
- Focus on your *upper back*, then completely relax it, and enjoy this comforting feeling.
- Focus on your *shoulders*, then completely relax them, and enjoy this comforting feeling.
- Focus on your *arms*, then completely relax them, and enjoy this comforting feeling.
- Focus on your *forearms*, then completely relax them, and enjoy this comforting feeling.
- Focus on your *wrists*, then completely relax them, and enjoy this comforting feeling.
- Focus on your *hands*, then completely relax them, and enjoy this comforting feeling.
- Focus on your *neck*, then completely relax it, and enjoy this comforting feeling.
- Focus on your *head*, then completely relax it, and enjoy this comforting feeling.
- Focus on your *mind*, then completely relax it, and enjoy this comforting feeling.

This last one is the most important. After you have focused on the present feeling of each and every physical body part, focus on "relaxing" your mind. This means disposing of any thoughts of yesterday and any thoughts of tomorrow.

You should now be in a much better state to fall asleep. Continue enjoying the present moment as much as possible, e.g., how the pillow feels on your face, how the blanket feels covering you, etc. Before you know it, you will be sleeping and wake up fully rested!

Success Review: Conquer Insomnia

Which previous *Success Strategy* did you notice while I was discussing this one?

Use the Power of Now

You probably noticed that I kept saying, "Focus on the present moment." This is essentially just using the *Power of Now* to fall asleep. Remember that the *Power of Now* helps you get rid of anxiety and worry by removing thoughts of the past and thoughts of the future. Once you are not worried, it is much easier to fall asleep.

Success Strategy: Conquer The Fear Of Death

To conquer the fear of death, stop thinking about when you will die. If you are always thinking about when you will die, you are actually dying right now. Your life becomes about death. Instead, make your life about enjoying life now rather than lamenting about a death that comes later.

What is the most common fear that people have? The fear of public speaking. But the fear of death is certainly in the top five most common fears that people have. While the fear of public speaking is easily overcome with practice of public speaking, the fear of death can't be overcome with practice … well, because you would die.

Most people argue that if you believe in God and an afterlife that there is no reason to fear death. However, people that believe in God are often more afraid of dying than even atheists are. Everyone wants to go to heaven, but no one wants to die to get there.

A more comforting mental hack to overcome your fear of dying is to focus on the present moment. Similar to conquering insomnia, thinking about the future does you no good. If you are constantly thinking about when you will die, then you miss out on all of the present moments that you could enjoy now. Essentially, you are letting yourself die today by living in the future.

Don't worry about whether you will die tomorrow because you will rob yourself of enjoying today.

Success Example: Conquer The Fear Of Death

I used to be scared to death of dying. My cousin first introduced to me to the concept of dying when I was just a child, maybe five or six years old. Sure, I had seen people die in movies, but I didn't know that people died in real life. Once I realized that my parents, my family, and I would all die, I freaked out.

I can remember one night, I ran into my parents' bedroom crying. I jumped on top of my dad sobbing and said, "I don't want you and mom to die. I want us to live for a million, billion years! I don't want to die!" My parents comforted me by assuring me that we would live for a very long time and that I had nothing to worry about.

Even as an adult, I used to fear death. On occasion, I have woken up in a terror because I had a nightmare about death. I would worry that there is just nothingness and no consciousness after death. It's still a scary concept.

But I don't let the fear of death bother me anymore. I now spend my day focusing on today, not tomorrow. Sure, I will have to eventually die. But if I spend all of my current moments thinking about that one moment of death, I've let death rob me of enjoying every other moment. Now, I don't waste my current moments worrying about death.

SUCCESS PRACTICE: CONQUER THE FEAR OF DEATH

Death happens tomorrow. Life happens today. If you spend your life focusing on death, then you let death happen today. To conquer your fear of death, simply enjoy the present moment of life as much as possible. Death cannot take your present enjoyment away from you.

SUCCESS REVIEW: CONQUER THE FEAR OF DEATH

Which previous *Success Strategy* did you notice while I was discussing this one?

Use the Power of Now

Once again, we can see how powerful the Power of Now is. Not only can it help you conquer insomnia, but it can also help you conquer the fear of death. Focusing on today, rather than yesterday or tomorrow, is the most powerful mental hack I know of to attain happiness. It's not what happens to you that determines your happiness; it's how you respond to what happens. Respond by focusing your thoughts on the current moment and accepting the present, and it's almost impossible to be unhappy.

Chapter 7
Marketing Success Strategies

(1) Sell Secrets
(2) Give Away Free Content
(3) Be Controversial
(4) Plant Viral Content
(5) Be Succinct
(6) Give People a Bigger Cause

Marketing Success Strategy #1
Sell Secrets

Success Strategy

One of the most effective ways to grab people's attention is to tell them you have a "secret." When you are marketing your product or service, you can pique interest by selling secrets.

A secret is a method, formula, or plan that is known to only a few. Secrets are intriguing because they imply exclusivity. If everyone knows a particular piece of information, then it loses its value. Secrets are also intriguing because they signal a competitive advantage to those that know them.

Books sell secrets all the time. In fact, the book *The Secret* is a manifestation of this strategy. This book intrigues people because they believe it holds exclusive knowledge that will give them a competitive advantage. Another example is Jeff Walker's #1 bestseller *Launch: An Internet Millionaire's Secret Formula To Sell Almost Anything Online, Build A Business You Love, And Live The Life Of Your Dreams.* Notice how Walker appeals to potential readers by stating that there is a "secret" formula to attaining things that essentially everyone wants—i.e., to live the life of their dreams. I also sell secrets in my books. For example, the tagline for my Prep Expert SAT books is "Perfect-Score Ivy League Student Reveals How to Ace The New SAT." Although I don't explicitly say "secrets," I certainly imply them by using the word "reveals."

Be careful when you "sell secrets." Do not sell empty promises. If you are going to tell people that you have a secret, you better give them something of value. As long as the knowledge you share has value to them, most people will not care how exclusive the content is. But if the information you give people is useless, then you will be accused of pushing lies and using click-bait.

Success Example

One of the most popular blog articles on PrepExpert.com was entitled "A Little-Known Secret About College Admissions." I've reproduced the article below. After reading it, you determine whether I offered semi-exclusive, useful knowledge to students. If so, then the title of the article is appropriate.

> *Want to get into the college of your dreams? Here's a little-known secret: impress the college's regional admissions officer to increase your chances.*
>
> *Colleges want students that want them. Colleges don't want to offer admission to a student who is not going to attend their institution. Therefore, qualified students who apply to universities without expressing any interest are often rejected.*
>
> *One of the best ways to express interest is to get to know your college's regional admissions officer. This is a full-time staff member at the admissions office who is assigned a certain geographic region, such as California, Nevada, and Arizona. This person will not only visit that geographic region during the fall, but will also be the first to read applications from his or her assigned area.*
>
> *If you have met the regional admissions officer for your geographic area, then he or she may advocate moving your application forward in the admissions process! So you should*

make it a point to build a relationship with them. For example, you may want to e-mail them, meet them when they visit your area, and even set up an interview on campus when you visit the university.

From my own experience, I really wanted to go to Brown University. As a senior in high school, I signed up for the lunch talk when the regional admissions officer visited our school. At a school of 3,000 students, I was the only student who signed up. Therefore, I was able to have a one-on-one chat with the regional admissions officer from Brown University about my interests and application to Brown. I also stayed in touch with her via e-mail throughout the admissions process. Fast-forward a few months, and I was admitted to Brown! While my grades and test scores certainly qualified for admission, I cannot help but believe that my personal relationship with the regional admissions officer helped me gain acceptance to this Ivy League university.

To give you another example, there was a couple at my high school who developed a good relationship with the regional admissions officer for Yale, and they both got in. Once again, I do believe that they were both qualified. However, I also think that having an advocate on your behalf in the admissions office can help your chances of acceptance tremendously!

You can start by e-mailing the admissions office of your desired university and finding out who the regional admissions officer for your geographic area is. Then, send this person an e-mail to find out if they will be visiting your region anytime soon. If you do have the chance to meet them in person, make a good first impression! It can be the difference between acceptance and rejection.

Success Practice

Let's have you start to sell secrets by writing a blog article. Here are the steps involved:

(1) Pick a topic that you are well informed about
(2) Identify something related to that topic that would be valuable to others (ideally, choose something that is not too commonly known)
(3) Write a blog post about what you know and call it "A Little-Known Secret About _____"
(4) Publish the blog post on your website, LinkedIn, Reddit, Facebook, Twitter, and other outlets
(5) Track page views to determine if selling secrets helped you generate more interest than usual related to your topic.

Expert marketers sell secrets!

Success Review

I practice what I preach!

This book's title is actually a manifestation of this strategy! The tagline to this book is, "Ivy League *Shark Tank* Entrepreneur Reveals 48 Secret Strategies To Live Happier, Healthier, and Wealthier." Notice how I connected "secrets" to items that everyone wants: to be happy, healthy, and wealthy. I am betting that selling secrets will help me sell more copies of this book.

Of course, my forty-eight "secrets" are really forty-eight strategies. Some of them are well-known and some of them are not. But I hope that they all add value to readers' lives. And because the secrets were not empty promises, I'm hoping people will be okay that I sold them secrets!

Marketing Success Strategy #2
Give Away Free Content

Success Strategy

People will not buy your product or service immediately because it is not the right time for them to purchase it. Do not lose these customer leads that may buy from you later. In order to do this, give them free content now so that you are top-of-mind when they are ready to make a purchase later.

Internet marketing has a golden rule: "Content is king." However, this is incorrect. It should be "Free content is king." In other words, you must be willing to give away some portion of your product or service in order to generate interest from potential customers.

The best way to do marketing on the Internet is not to do any marketing at all. In other words, don't yell at the top of your lungs that, "My product is the best in the world! You should try it because X, Y, and Z!" People don't respond to direct marketing—it's too obtrusive. Instead, you should try something like, "Download My Free Mini e-Book With The Top 10 Tips On How To X, Y, and Z." People will respond much better because they only care about free.

But there is no such thing as a free lunch. If you are giving away something highly valuable to potential customers, they should be willing to give you something: an e-mail address. You want to collect the e-mail addresses of potential customers because it allows you to communicate with them later with more free offers, tips, and eventually an offer to purchase your product or service.

SELF-MADE SUCCESS

SUCCESS EXAMPLE

When I was first starting Prep Expert, I had no idea what I was doing. I didn't have a clue about marketing, especially Internet marketing. I thought that if I just gave out flyers about my SAT classes to high schools that I would generate lots of marketing buzz. Boy, was I wrong. For the most part, high school counselors didn't really care about my SAT classes, especially since I hadn't even taught one SAT class yet for which I could show results.

One day while I was out for a morning run, I had a brilliant idea hit me—what if I gave away a free SAT essay e-book to students? I had previously been so protective about not releasing my content unless people paid for it. But what was the harm in giving away less than 10% of my paid content for absolutely free? There was none.

I set up a program that allowed people to download my SAT essay e-book for free if they liked Prep Expert on Facebook and wrote "Prep Expert Rocks!" on our company Facebook page. This resulted in over 1,000 new likes on our Facebook fan page, which showed social validation to others that we were a real company. More importantly, the free SAT essay e-book served as a lead generation tool. Once students and parents could see how effective my SAT essay strategies were, they were more inclined to purchase an SAT class from us.

Do not hide your content in a black box—give it away for free! People will appreciate it so much that they will become paying customers, as ironic as that sounds.

SUCCESS PRACTICE

Create a short 20- to 30-page e-book with ten tips related to a topic that you are an expert in. Now, release one of these tips each week on your website's blog. At the end of each blog post, write that people can download your free e-book by simply entering their e-mail into a form. You can use web tools such as LeadPages and MailChimp to capture e-mails. Make sure to get their permission to e-mail them later about more free tips and future offers.

If you don't want to create an e-book, you can also host a free webinar that people can register for to get tips and advice from you. You can use web tools such as ClickMeeting or GoToWebinar to host the webinar.

In any case, it doesn't really matter what content you give out (an e-book, webinar, etc.). Just make sure that it's relatively inexpensive for you to give out for free and that it's massively valuable for your potential customers. By building your e-mail list of potential leads, you will create a profitable business in no time.

Success Review

Which previous *Success Strategy* did you notice while I was discussing this one?

Realize that Million-Dollar Ideas Are Easy

Notice that my idea to give away a free SAT essay e-book to build my Facebook fan page following came to me when I was running. If you recall, I mentioned earlier that the best ideas often come to us when we are exercising because of dopamine release. Although the free SAT essay e-book was not a million-dollar idea in and of itself, it built a culture of giving away free content at Prep Expert, which has helped turn the company into a multi-million dollar business!

Marketing Success Strategy #3
Be Controversial

Success Strategy

In order to get noticed in a noisy world, you need to stand out. One way to separate yourself from the masses is to go against conventional wisdom. Be controversial to increase your click-through rate. Controversy is remembered; mediocrity is forgotten.

If you are controversial, you will get attention. Say something that others are afraid to say. However, make sure there is some truth to your position. Although people don't necessarily need to agree with you, you must have sound logic behind your unpopular opinion.

I first formally learned about this technique in James Altucher's *Choose Yourself!* In the book, Altucher encourages readers to take a contrarian view on topics. Altucher practices what he preaches. A couple weeks after I read his book, I saw a video on *Business Insider* that featured James Altucher entitled, "Warren Buffett is a f——g liar!" Talk about controversy. Most people view Warren Buffett as an intelligent investor who has a grandfather-like appeal. In the video, Altucher says things like, "Warren Buffet will slit your throat in a dark alley." He believes Buffett is lying when he says the average investor should hold stocks forever. Altucher claims that Buffett wants to take away the advantage of the average investor being able to make rapid trades so that Buffett is able to buy and sell his own stocks in large amounts more quickly. Now this is a very controversial opinion, but Altucher seems so convinced and passionate about it. In addition, his argument has some logic. So you can bet that this video got lots of views because of his controversial stance.

Be careful when practicing this strategy. Don't be so controversial to the point that it is embarrassing or dangerous. You should actually believe in your contrarian viewpoint. Don't do something that is wholly unethical or unlawful. Being controversial can help you stick out from the crowd, but it's not worth sacrificing your morals or principles for.

SUCCESS EXAMPLE

In high school, I wanted my valedictorian speech to be remembered. So I decided to be controversial (far before I had formally learned about this strategy). You can read my speech below.

> *I was going to stand up here today and talk about my biggest accomplishment during high school, which most of you may already know … how I brought sexy back. Unfortunately, that idea didn't make it past administration.*
>
> *So instead I want to tell you a story about this girl I met. I've known her for four years now and she's become my best friend. Although we've had some ups and downs in our relationship, she will always be in my heart and I will never forget her.*
>
> *When I first met this girl, I was unsure about how close we would eventually get. Many of my friends told me to stay away from her and instead pursue this other girl who seemed more attractive and lived closer to home. Plus, the first few times I really hung out with her, it didn't seem like she paid much attention to me because she already had so many other friends. Nevertheless, I stuck it out with her and am glad I did because as it turns out … I*

discovered that THIS girl is absolutely perfect for me.

She has introduced me to some of my best friends. I've spent most of my life for the past four years with this girl. I've had so much fun with her: we ran job fairs together, dissected cats together, had a senior barbecue, and she was even with me the night of Homecoming. Sometimes I would be with her from the early morning to late at night; four, five, even six days a week. But I've cherished every minute with this girl, and I love her with all my heart. I could not have been happier with any other girl.

However, the relationship I once had with this girl will never be the same because, one week ago ... (sigh) ... she died in my life. This girl's name ... ...

is Clark High School.

I hope my mom's blood pressure is back to normal now!

And so, we all share this one, common best friend: Clark. She has always been there for us unconditionally during our times of joy, pain, and excitement. Although she may have departed from our lives, her memory will live on. As we continue our journey through life, we shall never forget this friend whom all of us have come to know so intimately. Remember all that she has given us: what she has taught us, the friends she has introduced us to, the laughter and happiness she has brought us, and most importantly, the exceptional character she has brought out in each and every one of us.

Although I will be spending the next four years of my life with another girl, this one will always stay in my heart.

And so finally, I'd like to thank God, my parents, my family, and my friends for helping me to make the decision four years ago to take this road less traveled and meet this girl; because for me, it has made all the difference.

As you can see, my speech was rather controversial, or at least the first half was. I had to have a meeting with school administration who tried to prevent me from giving the speech. Luckily, I was able to make a good enough case that they let me deliver it.

Years later, I took further advantage of the speech. I put it on YouTube, with the title "Perfect SAT Score Student Dumps Girlfriend In Graduation Speech." Although the title is not entirely true, it certainly is controversial enough to get people to watch it. In fact, over 1.5 million people have watched the video and I still have people come up to me today to tell me about how they watched the speech online.

Be controversial to be remembered.

SUCCESS PRACTICE

There are multiple ways to be controversial. Here's one.

(1) Pick a topic that you are well-informed about.
(2) Identify a commonly-held belief related to that topic that you don't agree with.
(3) Write a blog post about why you don't agree with it and call it "Why _____ Is A Complete Lie!"
(4) Publish the blog post on your website, LinkedIn, Reddit, Facebook, Twitter, and other outlets.
(5) Track page views to determine if being controversial helped you generate more interest than usual related to your topic.

Expert marketers are controversial!

Success Review

Which previous *Success Strategy* did you notice while I was discussing this one?

Use the Art of Storytelling

Notice how my controversial valedictorian speech was in the form of a story. You can use stories that seem controversial at first, but actually reveal a surprising truth at the end. I also used the STAR Model we described in the Art of Storytelling:

> **Situation** — I'm unsure about whether I should date a girl
> **Task** — I need to decide whether the girl likes me too
> **Action** — I end up dating her and we have a great time
> **Results** — The girl was actually a metaphor for my high school

Marketing Success Strategy #4
Plant Viral Content

Success Strategy

Everyone wants to go viral. Viral growth can bring you wealth and fame. But it's difficult to predict what content will go viral. Or is it? Although most content goes viral organically, some content goes viral due to calculated planning by the producer. Planting viral content requires the content producer to anticipate how traditional media and social media will react to a certain piece of news.

Planting viral content requires two-step thinking: the first step is to understand how human emotions would be drawn to a certain piece of content, and the second step is to create content to capitalize on those emotions. The general public only engages in one-step thinking—i.e., believing the first headline it sees. Don't believe everything you see, especially Internet headlines.

Success Example

Here are three examples of planted viral content.

(1) Steve Harvey and Miss Universe

On December 20, 2015, Steve Harvey, the host of Miss Universe, announced the incorrect winner of the competition. Harvey announced that Miss Columbia, Ariadna Gutierrez, had won.

However, just a few minutes later, Harvey came back on stage to point out his mistake. Ariadna Gutierrez was actually the first-runner up in the competition, and Miss Philippines, Pia Alonzo Wurtzbach, was the winner of the competition. Harvey blamed this mistake on himself, stating that he simply misread the card. But was it really a mistake?

I believe the Miss Universe "mistake" was actually planted viral content. The Internet went nuts when it heard about Harvey's misstep. Miss Universe ratings had been falling for years. This was the perfect way for producers to drum up publicity for its dying franchise. In addition, the Miss Universe pageant is a live event. Typically, the winner isn't announced until the last two minutes of the program. In 2015, Harvey announced the winner with six minutes left—leaving plenty of time to correct the error and for the Internet to make Miss Universe go viral.

You might be thinking ... why would Steve Harvey want to look like an idiot in front of millions of people? The answer: publicity. Imagine the number of people who now know who Steve Harvey is after the incident. All publicity is good publicity. In addition, Steve Harvey was of course invited by producers to host the Miss Universe pageant again in 2016.

The producers and Steve Harvey clearly thought two steps ahead of the rest of the public with their planted viral content of "mistakenly" announcing the incorrect winner to the Miss Universe pageant.

(2) Ahmed Mohamed and The Clock Incident

On September 14, 2015, 14-year old Ahmed Mohamed wanted to bring a homemade clock to his high school in Irving, Texas to show his engineering teacher. Later that day, teachers and school administration called the police because they thought the clock was a homemade bomb. Mohamed was put in handcuffs and sent to a juvenile detention center. This was clearly discrimination against Muslims—at least that's what all of the headlines read. Or was it planted?

Mohamed and his family benefited hugely off of this publicity. They were invited to Facebook by Mark Zuckerberg, got invitations to top colleges such as MIT and Harvard, and even President Barack Obama tweeted "Cool clock, Ahmed. Want to bring it to the White House? We should inspire more kids like you to like science. It's what makes America great." Mohamed did meet the President at the White House.

But let's take a closer look at what happened. Mohamed claimed to have built the clock from scratch. But experts who examined the clock determined that it was simply a store-bought clock that Mohamed had placed in a silver pencil case that looked similar to a small briefcase—the kind that would house a home-made bomb.

After showing the clock to his engineering teacher in first period, Mohamed was advised to put the clock in his backpack for the rest of the day since it looked like a bomb. Not listening, Mohamed continued to show the clock to every teacher throughout the day. As a last ditch attempt, Mohamed decided to turn on a timer on the clock in his last class of the day. Only after the timer started beeping did his English teacher call the principal for further investigation. In addition, Mohamed was uncooperative, silent, and passive aggressive when the principal and police asked him questions about his homemade clock.

Then there's Mohamed's family background. His sister was suspended from school a year earlier for a similar bomb hoax. And the *Washington Post* wrote in 2011 that Mohamed's father "wears a cleric's flowing white robes and claims hundreds of followers throughout Egypt, Sudan and in the United States," and he often goes back to Sudan to run for President. In addition, after Mark Cuban spoke to Ahmed Mohamed, Cuban said, "I ask him a question, 'Tell me what happened,' because I'm curious, right? His sister, over his shoulder, you could hear, listening to the question, giving him the answer."

So this was likely a family plot for fame. And when the picture of "poor" Mohamed in handcuffs came out, the family had struck gold. Mohamed's family thought two steps ahead of the general public. First, they knew that the national media would love a story about an "innocent" Muslim teenager who was discriminated against. Second, they knew if they built a contraption that looked similar to a bomb that would later be revealed to be nothing more than a clock, they would go viral.

Interestingly, after more media began to pick up on the clock likely being a hoax, Mohamed and his family moved to Qatar.

(3) Drake Hotline Bling Video

On a much lighter note, planting viral content can also be used for entertainment and fun rather than national controversy. On October 19, 2015, music artist Drake released a video for his song, "Hotline Bling." The entire video is shot on a white background with Drake dancing by himself, both ridiculously and confidently.

Immediately, the Internet was flooded with memes of Drake's dance moves. The hilarious memes ranged from Drake making pizza to playing tennis. Although social media thought it was just making fun of Drake's dancing, it was actually making Drake's song go viral. Five days after the video came out, Drake's song peaked at #2 on the Billboard charts.

Of course, the memes were easy for the Internet to make because the whole video was shot on a white background. In addition, the goofy hand movements that Drake did throughout the video made it easy for social media to troll.

This certainly makes you wonder whether Drake and his team had known that the Internet would create memes out of the video. This was later confirmed by Drake's choreographer, Tanisha Scott, who said, "And all those memes and mashups—he knew that was going to happen." Drake masterfully used planted viral content to blow up his chart-topping single in 2015.

Success Practice

Now it's your turn to capitalize on planted viral content. If you're going to use it, there are two other rules you must follow when creating viral content.

First, your planted viral content can never be about you or your business. People don't care about you or your business, but they do enjoy seeing something funny, controversial, or ridiculous. Notice how the Steve Harvey mishap was not about the Miss Universe pageant. It was about how ridiculous Harvey's mistake was. The Ahmed Mohammed clock wasn't about his family, it was about prejudice against Muslims. Finally, even Drake's "Hotline Bling" memes weren't about his song, they were about how ridiculous his dance moves were.

Second, you can never reveal that you planned for your content to go viral by thinking two steps ahead of everyone else. People will feel manipulated, or worse, lied to. Steve Harvey will never admit that he purposely announced the wrong winner of Miss Universe. Ahmed Mohammed's family will never admit that they created a clock that looked very similar to a bomb in order to grab media attention. Finally, Drake won't admit that his ridiculous dance moves were intended to trick the Internet into doing the marketing for him.

Planted viral content is a powerful way to make you famous or even wealthy. Use it carefully!

Success Review

Which previous *Success Strategy* did you notice while I was discussing this one?

Give Away Free Content

Notice that all of the viral content examples I gave were free. You cannot go viral with paid content. Paid content such as *Game of Thrones* takes a while before it goes viral. And I'm guessing you don't have a reputation or marketing budget as big as HBO's. If you plan to be an Internet sensation, create free viral content!

Marketing Success Strategy #5
Be Succinct

Success Strategy

When you create content, keep it short. A short article, video, or pitch is more likely to be well-received than a long piece of content.

People have short attention spans, especially in today's world. They don't have time to give you fifteen minutes out of their day. This is why Twitter has been so successful—it forces content producers to limit themselves to 140 characters. Although you don't have to be that succinct when creating content, keep in mind that people do not want to dedicate a lot of time to you.

Short content is also important, given how people consume content. Sixty percent of all Internet traffic is mobile. So you have to keep in mind that people are reading your article, watching your video, or looking at your pictures on a small screen. In addition, it's so easy for them to exit your content as soon as they find it by just hitting the home button.

You might be happy to hear that you don't need to create long content for users because it seems like you will save time. However, I actually think it's more difficult to create content that's short than it is to create content that's long. When you are limited by length, you have to make sure that every part of your content is really impactful. There is no room for waste. For example, Vine is a social media video platform that limits content creators to six seconds. You might think that it would be easy to create such short videos.

But I'm sure if you talk to any top Viners, they will tell you that they spend hours and hours planning and recording the perfect six-second video.

Be succinct when creating content in order to create impactful content that won't bore people.

SUCCESS EXAMPLE

Being succinct is not only important when creating content, but it's also important when pitching ideas. For example, it was much harder to develop my one-minute *Shark Tank* open call audition pitch than it was to create my ten-minute *Shark Tank* audition video. For the open call audition, I had to really think about what words would make the biggest impact. For the video audition, I didn't have as much pressure to impress with every word.

On a side note, whenever you make a presentation, do not use notecards or a script. I have always found that my presentations—whether it's a pitch for a startup or a PowerPoint project for school—are much better when I don't try to memorize a script. I have noticed that people who try to stick to a script usually come off sounding more rigid than natural. With that being said, if you do create a script, be flexible. Do not force yourself to say every word perfectly. It's okay if you go off-script. No one knows what's on your script or if you "screwed up."

Here's the one-minute, succinct pitch that I gave at the open call audition for *Shark Tank* in New York City. Note that I didn't say this pitch word-for-word. Instead, I knew my main points really well and gave myself enough flexibility to go off-script so that I would sound as natural as possible.

(1) When I was in high school, I raised my SAT score from an average 1760 to a perfect 2400.

(2) Of the 15 million students who have taken the SAT, about 3,000 have gotten a perfect score—that's just .02%.
(3) Now, I'm the only one who went from average to perfect to start an SAT prep company: 2400 Expert.
(4) Based on my #1 bestselling SAT book, 2400 Expert is now the largest test prep provider in Las Vegas with over 10,000 students prepped.
(5) After a six-week class, the average score improvement is an industry-leading 368 points—with many of our students going to the Ivy League.
(6) We offer DOUBLE the course hours, at HALF the price, with TOP instructors.
(7) We've been featured in *The New York Times, USA Today,* and *Business Insider.*
(8) Now, 2400 Expert is looking to expand across the nation!
(9) So Sharks, who's ready to SCORE big off my perfect SCORE!?

SUCCESS PRACTICE

What is one pitch that almost everyone needs to create? A bio. You should create two forms of your bio: a short one and a long one. The short bio is more difficult to create than a long bio. So let's work on creating your short bio. Here are some questions to ask yourself:

(1) What do you consider yourself? (E.g., student, entrepreneur, consultant, etc.)
(2) What is the one item that you definitely want your relevant audience to know?
(3) What is an accomplishment that would be impressive to include?

When I ask myself these questions, here's how I would answer:

(1) Founder, Author, Student, Tutor
(2) I raised my SAT score from average to perfect and I wrote a #1 bestselling book about it
(3) I secured a deal with Mark Cuban on ABC's *Shark Tank*

Given the answers to the questions above, I put together the following short-form bio on my website:

Shaan Patel is the founder of Prep Expert Test Preparation, a #1 bestselling SAT prep author, an MD/MBA student at Yale and USC, and winner of an investment deal with billionaire Mark Cuban on ABC's *Shark Tank*. He raised his own SAT score from average to perfect and teaches students his methods in an online SAT prep class.

Notice how much information I was able to pack into two sentences. I made sure every word was important for my audience to know. Now it's your turn to create your short-form bio!

Success Review

Which previous *Success Strategy* did you notice while I was discussing this one?

Never Go to a Gunfight Without Bullets

When creating succinct content, every piece of it has to be impactful. For example, when you are creating a succinct pitch, you must show initial traction. Notice how I used every sentence of my open call audition to quickly impress my audience. Because it's going to be a short gunfight, you must fire your bullets quickly.

MARKETING SUCCESS STRATEGY #6
GIVE PEOPLE A BIGGER CAUSE

SUCCESS STRATEGY

The best marketing occurs when people don't know they are being marketed to. One way to do this is to connect people to a cause bigger than yourself.

People do not care about you or your business. People care about themselves. If you try to market by telling people about yourself and how great your product or service is, you will fail. Instead, connect your business to a cause that people care about.

I often am able to score media hits because I don't try to pitch the reporters about my company. Instead, I give them story ideas that their audience would care about. For example, here are three story ideas that I pitched to media reporters when the SAT changed from a 2400-scale back to a 1600-scale:

(1) 5 Tips to Prep for the New SAT from a Perfect-Score *Shark Tank* Entrepreneur
(2) *Shark Tank* Billionaire Mark Cuban Knows the SAT Is Changing. Do You?
(3) Why the SAT Is Changing & How It Benefits Students Everywhere

Notice how none of the story ideas mentioned my company, Prep Expert. Instead, they are all article titles that I thought the reporter's audience would genuinely be interested in. Of course, if a media reporter does agree to do one of the stories, they will include that I am the founder of Prep Expert, which is exactly what I wanted! But I don't say "Hey, do a story on my company Prep Expert!" You need to stop thinking about yourself and start thinking about causes that your audience cares about.

SUCCESS EXAMPLE

When I was set to air on *Shark Tank* in January of 2016, I had a marketing plan. I sent out the following e-mail to every high school principal in the country.

> *Hi Principal XXXXX,*
>
> *I'm excited to share the news that I will be airing on ABC's Shark Tank on Friday, January 29th to pitch my company 2400 Expert SAT Prep! To celebrate airing on Shark Tank, I would like to donate my New SAT Prep e-Book (which retails on Amazon for $9.99) to every student at _____ High School for free. Depending on the size of your school, this donation could be worth $20,000+. My previous book, McGraw-Hill's SAT 2400 in Just 7 Steps, sold over 30,000 copies and was a #1 bestseller on Amazon for SAT Prep.*
>
> *In exchange for the donation, I just ask that you send an e-mail to your high school asking them to watch Shark Tank on Friday, January 29th! We are trying to break the all-time record for most Shark Tank episode viewers: 8.6 million. Here is a short, two-minute video I put up on Facebook requesting users to share my video to help us break the Shark Tank record for most viewers (it's already gotten 20,000 views in two days):*
>
> *2400expert.com/shark-tank/*
>
> *With your help to spread the word about our airing, I hope we*

really can #breaktherecord!

Thanks,
Shaan

The e-mail worked! Hundreds of high school principals sent out e-mails to their parents and students to watch my episode. The plan worked for three reasons:

(1) I connected people to a cause bigger than myself (breaking the viewing record)
(2) I gave away free content (my SAT essay e-book)
(3) I made it easy for people to participate (just send an e-mail out)

Although we didn't break the viewing record because the previous season of *Shark Tank* was just too difficult to compete with, we did get 6.8 million people to watch our episode (compared to 5.6 million for the episode that aired the week before us). In addition, we got a huge part of our target demographic to watch (parents of high school students), which resulted in an even bigger *Shark Tank* Effect than expected!

SUCCESS PRACTICE

For the next marketing initiative that you take on, stop thinking about yourself or your business. Instead, think about what your audience cares about. By giving them a bigger cause that they are willing to support, you will find a much more responsive audience.

Try to find a free or low-cost way to connect your audience to a larger cause. In my case, it cost me nothing to give away an e-book (other than perhaps cannibalizing a few retail sales). But the marketing value of the exposure was priceless.

Success Review

Which previous *Success Strategy* did you notice while I was discussing this one?

Give Away Free Content

This was easy. I mentioned how I gave away free content to high school principals in the form of a free SAT essay e-book. People respond to free and retreat from paid. Do not try to sell anything. I also connected the principals to a cause bigger than myself—breaking the *Shark Tank* all-time viewing record. Combine free content with a big cause and you will exponentially increase the effectiveness of your marketing.

CHAPTER 8
ACADEMIC SUCCESS STRATEGIES

(1) Never Follow Your Passion
(2) Realize Repetition Is Not the Father of Learning
(3) Use Tiger Parenting
(4) Follow the Path of Least Resistance
(5) Master How to Study
(6) Go to College ... for Cheap

Academic Success Strategy #1
Never Follow Your Passion

Success Strategy

Do not follow your passion. Instead, follow what you are good at at the current moment.

I remember Steve Balmer, former CEO of Microsoft, energetically talking at my graduation from USC in 2011 about how students should follow their passion. He's not the only one espousing this "wisdom." So many career and academic advisors will tell you to find your passion before choosing a career, otherwise you'll be miserable at work. Perhaps that's why so many students spend so many extra years in college trying to figure out what they should study.

I have news for you: it doesn't matter. Your degree often has little bearing on the careers that you go into. I specifically say "careers" rather than "career" because you will have more than one kind of job in your life. Even if you plan to go into a highly specialized career, such as becoming a doctor or lawyer, you will likely also teach, write, conduct research, consult, and do many other activities beyond what may be traditional in your "career."

Mark Cuban is famous for saying, "Don't follow your passion; follow your effort." Essentially, do what you're good at. I can have a passionate desire for painting, but if I don't put the effort into becoming a great painter, I should not pursue that endeavor.

Millennial mindsets are too fluid to choose just one career for the rest of our lives. We often have multiple passions, so why choose one? Instead, focus on where you add the most value at the current point in time. The Internet also makes it possible to do more than one thing at one time. Do not limit yourself by following one passion.

SUCCESS EXAMPLE

My own career is a good example of this *Success Strategy*.

Am I passionate about test preparation, writing, teaching, entrepreneurship, medicine or business? My answer: I am passionate about all of them, but one does not outweigh the others. Instead, I have focused my attention on these different interests of mine at different points in my career. Specifically, I focus my career on one when I put a lot of time and effort into it.

I focused on test preparation when I was in high school studying for the SAT. I focused on writing when I was in college writing an SAT prep book. I focused on teaching after college when I taught my first Prep Expert courses. I focused on entrepreneurship when I was launching Prep Expert. I focused on medicine in medical school. I focused on business in business school.

Throughout my life, I have spread my time and effort across different disciplines. You do not need to be boxed into a single title. On *Shark Tank*, Lori Greiner asked me whether I wanted to be a doctor or an entrepreneur. She separated the careers into an "either/or" situation. Although I didn't think of it at the time, my answer should have been "both."

Success Practice

Ask yourself two questions:

(1) What am I passionate about?
(2) What have I put the most effort into?

If the answer to both of these questions is the same, great! You are part of the select few that can follow both their passion and their effort.

If the answer to the latter question is radically different than the answer to the former question, I suggest you pursue what you have put more effort into. Remember that time and effort is all that is required to have a competitive edge over the competition. If you have already put in the time and effort in one area, don't do a 180 and flip to another discipline. Instead, worry about dedication now, and passion later. In fact, the more time and effort you put into something, the more passionate you will become about it.

Success Review

Which previous *Success Strategy* did you notice while I was discussing this one?

Be Controversial

I purposely went for controversy with this strategy to make a point. When you take a viewpoint that is contrary to the masses, people will take notice. Because I took a stance that people should not follow their passion, this *Success Strategy* will likely stand out to readers. Be controversial and you will command attention.

Academic Success Strategy #2
Realize Repetition Is Not the Father of Learning

Success Strategy

The age-old adage, "Repetition is the father of learning" is incorrect. Instead, repetition via different perspectives is the father of learning.

I used to hate memorizing. I had to do it for SAT prep in high school. I had to do it for organic chemistry in college. I had to do it for microbiology in medical school. And I had to do it for operations in business school.

Memorization is no fun because you have to consciously try to memorize facts that you usually don't care much about. This can be especially difficult if the information that you are attempting to memorize is the same, over and over again.

In grade school, I developed my own memorization method based on the idea that repetition is the father of learning. My 7th grade science teacher told our class that if you see something seven times, you remember it. I have no idea whether this research is true. But I made it the basis of a memorization strategy I used throughout my education: The Seven Times Repetition Strategy. I would repeat the same information seven times, over and over, and try to memorize the information by brute force. While this would usually do the trick, it was not fun. It was an arduous and monotonous task.

In medical school, I discovered a better way to learn information: The Seven Perspectives Strategy. Instead of repeating the same information seven times over and over, it was far more effective to repeat the same information through seven different perspectives. For example, if I had to learn about Parkinson's disease, the old me would have read my same notes about the topic seven times over and over. However, the new me equipped with a new way to learn would read from seven different books about Parkinson's disease. Learning from various perspectives about the same topic was far more effective and less intensive than attempting to repeat the same information seven times, over and over.

Success Example

I did not realize that learning from multiple perspectives was the key to learning until late into medical school. Perhaps where this new learning method served me best was on the USMLE (United States Medical Licensing Exam). The USMLE is a three-part exam required to practice medicine in the United States that tests anatomy, behavioral sciences, biochemistry, microbiology, pathology, pharmacology, physiology, and interdisciplinary topics such as nutrition, genetics, and aging.

I took the USMLE Step 1 exam after my second year of medical school. At this point, I was still stuck using my Seven Times Repetition Memorization strategy. It was a horrible experience. I would spend twelve hours a day repeating the same material over and over again. I could not stand it. Eventually the notes that I had created were imprinted in my brain, but it was not fun getting there.

I took the USMLE Step 2 exam after my third year of medical school. At this point, I had discovered the power of different perspectives. Instead of brute force memorization like I had used to study for the USMLE Step 1, I migrated my study strategy to reading as many books as possible (over 30 plus in total) related to the USMLE Step 2. This would assure that I would see the same topics covered at least seven times, but in different ways. This method worked so much better than going over the same material over and over! I actually looked forward to studying. It was no longer an arduous struggle of memorization, but a simple task of reading without worrying about information assimilation—it happened naturally.

Needless to say, I scored better on the USMLE Step 2 than I did on the USMLE Step 1 (most students do). More importantly, studying for the USMLE Step 2 was not nearly as taxing and difficult as it was studying the USMLE Step 1 because I focused on gathering as many different perspectives as I could related to the same topic.

SUCCESS PRACTICE

The next time you need to learn something for school, do not rely on just one source of information. Instead, find seven different sources of information and read them all. You will find that reading different perspectives on the same subject will help you really learn the information, rather than just memorizing it for a day.

In addition, reading different perspectives on the same topic will give you depth of knowledge on a topic that is far beyond that which you would have gotten by relying on one source of information. You will make connections that you didn't see before. You will find explanations in one source that clarify many of the questions you had about a topic when you were reading about it in a different source. Finally, you will understand what's really important to know about a topic as you will see commonalities among the various sources.

Success Review

Which previous *Success Strategy* did you notice while I was discussing this one?

Work Smarter and Harder

The Seven Perspectives Strategy is a manifestation of working harder and smarter. This learning technique requires you to work harder because you are gathering information from more sources than most other people would. It also requires you to work smarter because you are not relying on just one source of information for all of your knowledge related to a subject.

Academic Success Strategy #3
Use Tiger Parenting

Success Strategy

Amy Chua's 2011 book *The Battle Hymn of the Tiger Mother* caused quite the stir with its premise that strict parenting leads to better academic and disciplinary outcomes for children. But I fully agree with this premise.

I certainly had "tiger" parents growing up. My dad in particular was very strict about grades. Getting a "B" in a class was simply unacceptable. He made sure that I was very focused on my studies, always. In my family, education came first. However, my dad's family did not place such a big emphasis on education. My dad's parents had no schooling and lived in a village in India.

But my dad had the good fortune of the high school principal taking my dad under his wing. The high school principal practiced tiger parenting on my dad. He saw potential in my dad, and anything less than excellence was simply unacceptable. This helped my dad leave the village and become a pharmacist. Education was the key to changing my dad's life for the better. And so he expected nothing less than excellence in education from both my brother and me.

My parents instilled fear in me from an early age. I can remember as a young child in elementary school practicing my handwriting with my dad. After multiple attempts of not writing within the lines, my dad yelled at me for being incompetent. I began crying.

While this may sound cruel, I think some tough love (especially from an early-age) is necessary.

Eventually, I became conditioned to expect excellence from myself. I learned that if I did well in school, I could have a lot more freedom. My parents would not be breathing down my neck and I wouldn't have to have arguments with them about not getting an A. So get an A, and all would be fine. By the time I got to high school, I had learned my lesson. Just work really hard to assure that I get an A in every class, and I won't have to worry about my parents. This is when external motivation turned into internal motivation. I stopped getting A's because my parents wanted me to, and started getting A's because I wanted to. I eventually became valedictorian of my high school. So did my brother.

I believe that tiger parenting can have profoundly positive effects on a child. Not only will a child do well in academics, but he or she will apply those principles of hard work and discipline to his or her career as well.

SUCCESS EXAMPLE

I was so afraid of my parents that I went to great lengths to erase any academic blemishes from my high school record. In middle school, I got a B in my Spanish class. However, this wasn't just any Spanish class. This was a Spanish class that gave you high school credit, to my detriment. It wouldn't have been a big deal if the class was just for middle school, but this particular class was going to go on my high school transcript.

Having a B on my high school transcript before I even started high school would ruin my chances of becoming valedictorian. That's when a counselor came into our class to inform us that if we retook Spanish I in high school, the grade that we got in our middle school Spanish class would be erased from our record.

So that's exactly what I did. During freshman year of high school, I enrolled in both Spanish I and Spanish II at the same time. I was taking Spanish I in order to erase the B I had gotten in middle school and taking Spanish II to continue fulfilling my language requirement without any missteps.

My parents never saw the B that I got in middle school Spanish because I luckily was able to get the report card from the mailbox before they could. Although they asked me about it for a while, eventually they forgot or maybe just assumed that I had gotten all A's. My parents also never knew that I retook Spanish I in high school to wipe away the B I had gotten in Spanish I in middle school. All they knew was that I was valedictorian. But my "valedictorian" status should have an asterisk.

Nevertheless, this traumatic experience kicked my butt into shape. As an 8th grader in middle school, I was still not fully disciplined about school. But as a 9th grader who had to go to great lengths to hide and erase a B from my high school transcript, I learned my lesson. I would never get a B in another high school class again, no matter what.

Success Practice

If you are a parent, be stricter about your student's grades. Try to point out how hard you worked in school (or if you didn't work hard in school, how hard you work now) to try to set a good example. My dad would always tell me about how he would get the highest grades in his class in India. It helps your child develop an archetype to aspire to.

If you are a student, listen to your parents. They are often the only people in this world who love you unconditionally. They only want what's best for you. Although tiger parents may seem cruel, there is a method to their madness. And you will only be able to appreciate it later in life.

Success Review

Which previous *Success Strategy* did you notice while I was discussing this one?

Be Controversial

I purposely went for controversy with this strategy to make a point. When you take a viewpoint that is contrary to the masses, people will take notice. Because I took a stance that people should use tiger parenting, this *Success Strategy* will likely stand out to readers. Be controversial and you will command attention.

Academic Success Strategy #4
Follow the Path of Least Resistance

Success Strategy

Follow the path of least resistance to avoid working hard when you don't have to. Work hard when you need to, but be lazy when you can. Become the hardest working lazy person you know.

I work very hard ... when it counts. I worked very hard in high school to make sure that I got an A in every class so that I could be become valedictorian and get into BS/MD medical programs. I worked very hard in college to write my first SAT prep book and launch Prep Expert. I worked very hard in medical school to study for the USMLE. I worked very hard in business school to scale my business nationwide.

However, I don't work hard when it doesn't count. I followed the path of least resistance in high school by dropping two classes my last semester because I had already applied to college and had enough credits to graduate. I followed the path of least resistance in college by taking the easiest electives possible (e.g., Hip-Hop Music & Culture) so that I could have time to write my book and launch my business. I followed the path of least resistance in medical school ... well actually there was no path of least resistance in med school—I just worked really hard. I followed the path of least resistance in business school by stacking all of my classes on Tuesdays and Thursdays so that I could spend the rest of my time scaling Prep Expert.

Notice how while I was working very hard in some ways, I was also being very lazy in other ways. You need to learn the rules of the game first—figure out what matters and what doesn't. Then, you need to play the game better than anyone else. Too many people work hard at everything and burn out. This is not the most efficient way to work. Follow the path of least resistance for activities that don't contribute to helping you achieve your goals.

Success Example

The Baccalaureate/MD program that I was enrolled in at the University of Southern California had one rule regarding the MCAT (Medical College Admissions Test). In order to be guaranteed acceptance into medical school at USC, students must score a 27 (out of 45) on the MCAT, but there was no minimum score required on the writing (essay) section.

Given the rules of the game above, did you see where you could potentially follow the path of least resistance? On the MCAT writing section. Technically, you would not have to try very hard on the writing portion of the MCAT since the Baccalaureate/MD program did not require a minimum score.

So I took this to the extreme. I did not do the writing section of the MCAT at all. I spent the entire hour that was supposed to be dedicated to writing an essay resting my eyes (I had gotten very little sleep the night before). I'm sure that I could have written an awesome essay simply by using my SAT essay template (I did this for the GMAT writing section and got a perfect score). But why bother? I followed the path of least resistance by not taking the writing section at all.

When I got my MCAT score, my writing score was an "X" even though it is supposed to be graded on a scale from J through T. But it didn't matter because the rules of my program did not require a specific writing score. Even though I followed the path of least resistance, USC still kept their word of guaranteeing me acceptance into medical school because I played within the rules.

Success Practice

One tangible way to use this strategy is to create a path of least resistance. You can do this in any class that you take in high school, college, or graduate school. Simply put in extra early effort at the beginning of the quarter or semester. By working hard early, your teacher will be impressed early on. This will give you some flexibility to coast later on because your teacher will have some good will towards you from your positive first impression. You have just created a path with less resistance for you to get a high grade in any course.

They say it takes about seven seconds for someone to make a first impression of you. I believe it takes about seven classes for your teacher to make a first impression of you as a student. Within your first seven classes, make sure that you raise your hand to ask and answer questions, turn in well-written papers or assignments, and talk to the teacher after class about topics he or she is teaching. By putting in the extra effort early, you have just allowed yourself to have more flexibility later during the course to not work as hard as you initially did and still get an A.

Success Review

Which previous *Success Strategy* did you notice while I was discussing this one?

Work Smarter and Harder

Following the path of least resistance is essentially the "Work Smarter" part of Work Smarter and Harder. However, notice that you should not follow the path of least resistance with respect to everything you pursue. If you have a goal that you really want to achieve, then you must work extremely hard for it. Do not follow the path of least resistance for goals that mean a lot to you.

Academic Success Strategy #5
Master How to Study

Success Strategy

The problem with school is that everyone tells you to "study," but no one teaches you how to study. Here are five tangible techniques that I use that massively improve my ability to study.

Study Tip #1: Start With The Hardest

"Studying" can entail many different tasks. Start with the hardest task first. For example, when I was studying for the SAT, I would always begin with memorizing vocabulary words. Memorizing vocabulary words was the most taxing on my brain. Therefore, I would start with this task first since my mind is freshest at the beginning of a studying session.

Study Tip #2: Time Tasks

Put a time limit on the tasks you need to complete. For example, when I was studying for the USMLE Step 1, I knew that reading 20 pages of a medical study guide took me about one hour. If I started reading at noon, I would try to have twenty pages read by 1:00 p.m. Timing your tasks will keep you on track.

Study Tip #3: Take Breaks

Ironically, one of the best ways to stay focused is to take breaks. You cannot concentrate for more than an hour or two at a time. So you should build in time to your study schedule to take breaks. For example, I typically schedule out four-hour study blocks but after one hour of studying, I reward myself by allowing myself to check text messages, e-mail, Facebook, etc. After two hours of studying, I usually take a lunch or snack break. I then try to do a difficult task after eating since my brain has newfound energy from the food.

Study Tip #4: Introduce Study Variation

Reading for four hours straight is very difficult. Instead, break up each hour of studying with different tasks. For example, here is an example of a study schedule I suggest for my SAT students:

Hour 1	Memorize Vocabulary Words
Break	10 Minutes
Hour 2	Read New SAT Strategies
Break	10 Minutes
Hour 3	Review Old SAT Strategies & Questions
Break	10 Minutes
Hour 4	Practice SAT Questions

Notice how my students never do the same thing for more than an hour. This variation makes four hours of studying much more bearable. I also run my three-hour SAT classes in the same way. Although most parents are initially nervous about their student being able to sit through a three-hour SAT class, students usually compliment us about how fast time flies. It's because we're constantly varying the schedule of the class in the following way:

40 Minutes	Vocab Quiz & Homework Review
45 Minutes	SAT Lesson Part 1
10 Minutes	Break
45 Minutes	SAT Lesson Part 2
40 Minutes	Test Review

Study Tip #5: Study At The Library

Study at the library if you want to be extremely efficient. After all of these years of studying for various exams, I've learned that one location is the most conducive to concentrated studying—the library. There is simply no better place to study.

Home is full of distractions. At home, not only is there an abundance of technology around (computers, laptops, TVs, etc.), but there are also non-tech distractions—your brother, your mother, your dog, etc.

Home is typically too comfortable of a setting to study in. The library on the other hand, has very few distractions. You can't talk in the library. If you keep your wireless Internet off at the library, you can avoid most technology. There are no TVs at the library. There are no family interruptions at the library. The library is pretty much the most boring place on the planet. And that is why the library is the perfect place to study.

Of course, I understand that not everyone has a library readily accessible that they can study at. In that case, you want to create an environment that is as similar to a library as possible. This means a large desk space that is free of clutter, a quiet area where you will not be distracted by others, sufficient lighting so that you are not squinting when reading, an office chair (studying in your bed is just too comfortable), and most importantly a technology-free environment.

SUCCESS EXAMPLE

Every major studying task that I have ever completed has been done at the library. I likely picked up this habit because the front office at a budget motel in urban Las Vegas was not the most conducive place to study. So I would almost always go to the library to study instead. I have carried this habit with me through high school, college, medical school, and business school.

In high school, I studied for the PSAT, SAT, AP Exams, and SAT Subject Exams at the library. In college, I studied for the MCAT at the library. In medical school, I studied for the USMLE exams at the library. Before business school, I studied for the GMAT at the library. I truly believe that my relatively good scores on most of these exams are attributable to me being able to put in ultra-concentrated effort at the library.

Success Practice

I have a challenge for you. Spend two hours at the library doing concentrated study. Then, spend two hours at home doing concentrated study. Compare how effective the studying at each location was.

Did you get more studying done at the library then at home? Did you get distracted less at the library compared to home? Did you seem to absorb the information better at the library then at home?

My guess is that the answer to all of these questions will be yes! Take the challenge—if it doesn't work for you, you can say you proved me wrong. But if it does work for you, your academic life just changed ... for the better!

Success Review

Which previous *Success Strategy* did you notice while I was discussing this one?

Turn Off the Tech

I mentioned that home is often not the best place to study because of all the technology. If you want to Master How to Study, you must Turn Off the Tech. These days, it's so easy to be distracted by technology: e-mail, text messaging, Facebook, Instagram, Twitter, and Snapchat. When I study for a standardized exam, I turn off the Internet, silence my cell phone, and study from print books. I am amazed by how much more work I am able to accomplish without all of the technological distractions.

ACADEMIC SUCCESS STRATEGY #6
GO TO COLLEGE ... FOR CHEAP

SUCCESS STRATEGY

You should go to the best college possible for the lowest cost possible. Do not take on a huge debt burden for a post-secondary education.

This is a huge debate. Do you need a college education to succeed in today's society? Many entrepreneurs would say "no," citing that there is enough free online education to teach you anything that you need to know to succeed. While this may be true, what are the chances that you will succeed in leveraging these resources appropriately? Working hard won't guarantee success. You are taking a huge risk by skipping college and going straight to work. Reduce this risk by going to college and getting at least a bachelor's degree.

Perhaps I have this view of the world because I grew up in a budget motel around people that had nothing but a high school education and I saw how bad life was for them. Sure, there are stories of people who grew up to be millionaires or even billionaires with nothing but a high school education. But that is the exception, not the norm.

The truth is the job market is fierce. When I put up a job posting for Prep Expert for a position as an instructor or proctor, I am flooded with applications. If an applicant doesn't have a college education, I usually don't move them forward to the next round in the application process. I believe many employers behave the same way. A college degree is the bare minimum for many jobs these days. Without one, it's often difficult for an employer to judge your qualifications. This is the same reason I don't believe standardized testing will ever be eliminated from the college admissions process. Colleges need a quick and dirty way to separate the good from the bad, and so do employers. Colleges use SAT and ACT scores and employers use level of education.

With that being said, college is expensive. I would suggest that you try to go to the best college you can for as cheap as possible. Mark Cuban certainly followed this line of thought when he chose to attend Indiana University strictly based on its low tuition. Use whatever means possible—apply for need-based grants and merit-based scholarships; get a part-time job; or start a business, to make sure that you don't come out of school in significant debt.

Go to college ... for cheap.

Success Example

When I applied to college, I got into some great universities—Brown, Berkeley, and Johns Hopkins. However, what I really wanted was to get into a BS/MD program. And I got into some great ones—USC, Northwestern, Boston University, and Villanova.

At the end of the day, I did not care about the prestige of Brown, Berkeley, or Johns Hopkins. I just cared about going to a medical program so that I could relax during undergrad and not have to worry about medical school admissions. So it came down to choosing between Northwestern's BS/MD program and USC's BS/MD program.

Although Northwestern's BS/MD program is certainly more well-known and prestigious than USC's BS/MD program, I chose USC for one reason: the money. USC offered a full-tuition scholarship and Northwestern didn't offer any scholarships. I could either go to Northwestern for $150,000+ or go to USC for free. The choice was simple—fight on!

The high-cost of medical school at USC was actually the impetus that led me to create Prep Expert my senior year of college. I needed a way to fund my upcoming medical school education. I have been lucky enough that Prep Expert has been profitable enough for me to fund my graduate education.

I understand that not everyone has this luxury. But you must find a way to go to the best schools that you can for the lowest price possible. I have heard of physicians that graduated from Johns Hopkins medical school 30 years ago who are still paying off their medical school loans. Stay away from being in debt your whole life—go to college … for cheap.

SUCCESS PRACTICE

This tip is to help high school students (or their parents) make college as cheap as possible. Note that most scholarships are only offered to high school seniors, but freshmen, sophomore, and juniors can always start getting ready early!

When I was in high school, I received over $80,000 in private scholarships from companies like Coca-Cola, Toyota, and McDonald's. This meant that not only was my tuition free at USC, but my housing, food, textbooks, and all other school-related expenses were paid for as well. I did not pay a dime to go to one of the most expensive private universities in the country!

Many people attribute my scholarship success to my perfect SAT score. While having a stellar SAT score certainly helped, there was one simple secret that helped me secure a debt-free college experience: local scholarships are easier to win.

The fewer applicants there are to a particular scholarship, the greater your chances are of winning that scholarship. And local scholarships undoubtedly have fewer applicants than national scholarships. For example, if you apply to a scholarship that is only open to students in your state, then the competition has already been reduced by at least 50 times.

Of the one hundred scholarships I applied to during my senior year of high school, I only won one national scholarship that was open to everyone. However, I won over twenty local scholarships, which were only open to students in my community, city, or state. This means that applying for those national scholarships is actually a waste of time. In order to find local scholarships, you will have to do some legwork.

(1) Visit The Counselor's Office — Your high school counselor will likely be a resource for local community scholarships. Companies often announce a scholarship they are offering by notifying high school counselors. But sometimes, that message doesn't get relayed to students. So make sure you pay a visit to your college counselor.

(2) Research Online — You can find many local scholarships by doing quick searches online. For example, if you go to high school in Burbank, California, search for terms such as, "California Scholarships," "Burbank Scholarships," "Los Angeles Scholarships," and "Southern California Scholarships." You will quickly find scholarships you've never heard of before. And that's good! The more obscure the scholarship, the fewer applicants it is likely to have.

(3) Ask Around — When we live in the age of laptops, iPhones, and iPads, we sometimes forget one of the best ways to obtain information: word of mouth. Often times, older high school students know of scholarships that are specific to your community and school. Ask around in your community if anyone knows of any scholarships offered by local companies.

(4) Apply For National Local Scholarships — What is a "national local" scholarship? Well, I just made up the term. But I define it as "a national scholarship that allocates a certain number of scholarships to each state or community." For example, when I was in high school, I applied for an award called the AXA Achievement Scholarship. Although it was a national scholarship in association with U.S. News and World Report (so everyone knew about it), I still believed I had a good shot at winning. Why? Because even though the scholarship was open to everyone in the nation, AXA gave a $10,000 scholarship to one student in every state. Essentially, this "national" scholarship was turned into a "national local" scholarship. I figured I had a good shot at winning because of this. And I was right!

(5) Find Local Scholarship Foundations — Look for foundations in your community that are dedicated to disbursing scholarships. When I attended school in Las Vegas, there was an organization called the "Clark County Public Education Foundation (CCPEF)". The sole purpose of this organization was to give out scholarships to students. There are lots of individuals, organizations, and companies that want to give money to the youth. However, these donors don't always know how to start their own scholarship program. So instead, they hire organizations like CCPEF to create, manage, and disburse scholarships on their behalf. CCPEF had a database of hundreds of scholarships that were only open to Las Vegas students. Prep Expert actually gives scholarships to Las Vegas high school students through CCPEF. See if there is a similar organization in your community.

Once you have identified which local scholarships you will be applying for, it's time to really focus on your applications. Put the deadlines for each scholarship in your planner so that you don't forget. And make sure you work weeks in advance to put together the best possible application (especially the essay). By putting together stellar applications for many local scholarships, you are almost guaranteed to win!

SUCCESS PRACTICE

Which previous *Success Strategy* did you notice while I was discussing this one?

Practice Dhandho Philosophy

Recall that Dhandho Philosophy is a low-risk, high-reward approach to life. In this case, going to college reduces the risk of being jobless and going for cheap increases the reward (because you are not in significant debt). Try to go to the best college possible to increase your reward as much as possible, but do not go if it will leave you in significant debt since that would increase your risk substantially.

Conclusion

Thank you for reading all the way to the end of this book! I know your time is valuable. You could have spent it doing a million other things. But you chose to spend it reading my words. I appreciate your taking the time to listen.

I know we have covered a lot of ground on a wide variety of topics. But I want to make sure you get a return on your investment. So let's just focus on implementing one strategy in your life—your favorite one. To do this, fill in the blanks below.

My favorite *Success Strategy* was
_____
I liked this *Success Strategy* because
_____
I will use this *Success Strategy* by
_____
Because of this *Success Strategy*, next year I am
_____

I purposely wrote the last fill-in-the-blank sentence in present tense in order to help you *Use the Law of Attraction* — my personal favorite *Success Strategy*.

Self-Made Success

By focusing on implementing just one *Success Strategy*, the 47 others will follow by domino effect. I hope this will result in a life that truly is happier, healthier, and wealthier.

Author's Note

I hope you enjoyed the book! This was my first attempt at writing a self-help book. Let me know what you thought by e-mailing me at shaan@prepexpert.com

Give this book away! Share this book with a friend whom you think could benefit from one or more of the strategies in this guide.

Check out the online course! If you liked the book, let's take your success to the next level. I have developed an online course that expands on the strategies in this book. Find out more at PrepExpert.com

Made in the USA
Middletown, DE
13 April 2017